Carol Du

MW00667697

What CEOs and Board Members are Saying about
Great Companies Deserve Great Boards

"A powerful resource for CEOs and board members packed with relevant, real-life examples."

—Joe Herring, Chairman and CEO, Covance

"Crisply written and chock-full of insights for CEOs and board members."

—Leonard Coleman, former President,
National League of Professional Baseball
and Presiding Director, Avis-Budget Group

"I highly recommend Great Companies Deserve Great Boards as an excellent read for CEOs, directors and others... Beverly Behan has consulted far and wide in preparing this comprehensive book."

—Frank Brown, Dean, INSEAD

"A well-written book from an author who has grappled with the challenges of the boardroom. Contains penetrating insights into the CEO/Board dynamic; offers clear and refreshingly pragmatic recommendations for more effective boards."

—Gail Cook-Bennett, Chair of the
Board, Manulife Financial

"I get a great deal of board practices material from a variety of well-regarded sources and this is the single best piece I have read."

—Wendy Lane, board member, Willis Group,
Laboratory Corporation of America, UPM-Kymmene

"Beverly Behan has created an outstanding resource in *Great Companies Deserve Great Boards*. It's not enough that boards strive to meet obligations. Every company deserves a great board that adds value to the company and makes the CEO a better leader. Beverly has put her two decades of hands-on board experience to work to do just that."

—Carol Stephenson, Dean, Richard Ivey School of
Business and active board member of
several Canadian and US boards

"Bev hits the nail on the head! Pragmatic and filled with tactics and approaches that really work."

—Don Shippar, Chairman and former CEO, ALLETE, Inc.

"Engaging and thought-provoking from the very outset. Soon I was underlining pages for quick future reference. An insightful and valuable handbook for not only CEOs but for all directors."

—Joel L. Reed, Lead Director, Venoco, Inc

"A must-read for new CEOs and those executive who aspire to be competitive for a CEO assignment."

—Mike Bonney, President and CEO,
Cubist Pharmaceuticals, Inc.

"How a Board of Directors operates can make or break a CEO. For those CEOs who want to be in the first category, this book is a 'must-read.'"

—James R. Ukropina, former Lead Director
of a Fortune 100 company

"*Great Companies Deserve Great Boards* is a practical primer for CEOs who want to maximize the effectiveness of their boards. Delivers advice on how to transform the corporate board into a significant strategic asset while avoiding the pitfalls that plague so many boards today."

—Susan Ness, former Federal Communications
Commissioner and board member.

"*Great Companies Deserve Great Boards* serves as an indispensable tool and roadmap of the do and don't in the world of boards. Written in a easy to read 'plane time' format, it provides excellent examples of the author's teachings and recommendations. The valuable insight gained from this publication are enormously worthwhile for anyone who is on or works with boards."

—Gary D. Cohen, Chief Administrative
Officer and Secretary, The Finish Line, Inc.

"*Great Companies Deserve Great Boards* is a must read for not only CEO's but all board members and senior executives. Beverly Behan shows that she really gets it when it comes to board operations."

—Tim Marquez, Founder, CEO and
Chairman of the Board, Venoco, Inc.

"Bev Behan has provided the definitive guide on how to fully reap the benefits of a Board of Directors and create a brain trust, a partnership, and a winning team for the company and shareholders."

—Leslie Kenne, Lieutenant general (retired)
US Air Force, Board Member of both
public and not-for-profit companies

"Bev Behan's extensive experience working with boards and executives is evident in this book. The concepts presented are sound, simple, and essential for successful board operations. As a new CEO and chairman, I found her book to be very helpful and recommend it highly for board members, CEOs, executives, and anyone that deals with corporate governance."

—John C. Procario, Chairman, President and
CEO, American Transmission Company

GREAT COMPANIES DESERVE GREAT BOARDS

A CEO'S GUIDE TO THE BOARDROOM

BEVERLY BEHAN

palgrave
macmillan

GREAT COMPANIES DESERVE GREAT BOARDS
Copyright © Beverly Behan, 2011.

All rights reserved.

First published in 2011 by
PALGRAVE MACMILLAN®
in the United States—a division of St. Martin's Press LLC,
175 Fifth Avenue, New York, NY 10010.

Where this book is distributed in the UK, Europe and the rest of the world,
this is by Palgrave Macmillan, a division of Macmillan Publishers Limited,
registered in England, company number 785998, of Houndmills,
Basingstoke, Hampshire RG21 6XS.

Palgrave Macmillan is the global academic imprint of the above companies
and has companies and representatives throughout the world.

Palgrave® and Macmillan® are registered trademarks in the United States,
the United Kingdom, Europe and other countries.

ISBN: 978–0–230–11365–7

Library of Congress Cataloging-in-Publication Data

Behan, Beverly.
    Great companies deserve great boards : a CEO's guide to the
    boardroom / by Beverly Behan.
        p. cm.
        ISBN 978–0–230–11365–7
        1. Boards of directors. 2. Corporate governance. I. Title.

HD2745.B45 2011
658.4'22—dc22   2010049706

A catalogue record of the book is available from the British Library.

Design by Newgen Imaging Systems (P) Ltd., Chennai, India.

First edition: June 2011

10 9 8 7 6 5 4 3 2 1

Printed in the United States of America.

With Thanks...

First and foremost to my parents, John and Trudy Behan,
my best friends for fifty years, who gave me their
unwavering support when I told them that
I wanted to quit practicing law to work with Boards of Directors.

Second, to the many wonderful clients, colleagues and friends
who have shared their boardroom issues and their friendship
with me over the years and have taught me much about both.

CONTENTS

ILLUSTRATIONS

PREFACE

WHEN I WAS IN MY EARLY THIRTIES, I had my first exposure to working with Boards of Directors. I saw talented, accomplished people sitting around mahogany board tables contributing very little—and I was shocked. In 1994, the Toronto Stock Exchange published a report by a commission led by Peter Dey called "Where Were the Directors?" It was a scathing rebuke of the dismal state of corporate governance in Canada. And I read it on a beach in Vancouver—where I was living at the time—like it was a racy novel. It served to confirm many of the disturbing things I had begun to realize about the way boards functioned.

Shortly afterward, I made a decision to start working with Boards of Directors—not in terms of a legal compliance focus, which my law firm at the time was keen to have me do. Instead, I wanted to learn how to make boards a genuine asset for the companies they governed. In 1996, I joined the executive compensation practice at William M. Mercer in Vancouver as a means of gaining greater experience on the front lines in working with boards. From the beginning, I wanted to expand my board work well beyond executive compensation (which, frankly, I didn't care for at all) and get into meatier issues. Fortunately, a shareholder activist named Yves Michaud targeted the major Canadian banks with a series of shareholder proposals, and my then-boss, who was the executive compensation consultant to the Bank of Montreal, brought me in on the broader governance issues. From there, I had the opportunity to work with BMO's board for three years on board and director evaluation and other initiatives for which their board won both national and international recognition.

In 2000, I was transferred to New York to work with Mercer Delta Consulting, a division of Marsh & McLennan that wanted to develop a board consulting practice. At this point, I gave up my executive compensation work entirely and focused on board effectiveness issues—which has been my focus ever since. If anyone would have told me back in 1995, when I was poring over the Dey Report on a Vancouver beach, that I would be working in New York at the time of the fall of Enron, I would never have believed it. Suddenly, corporate governance became a mainstream business issue—and I had the extreme good fortune to be in the right place at the right time. I was also blessed with colleagues and clients in New York who enabled me to learn more in the boardroom every day and gave me the opportunity to coauthor my first book on this topic *Building Better Boards: A Blueprint for Effective Governance* (Jossey-Bass, 2005).

In 2006, I left Mercer Delta and joined the Hay Group, which enabled me to expand my board work internationally. Within a month after joining Hay, I was in a boardroom in Tel Aviv. The following year we held a governance forum in New York for directors and executives of companies in China. Shortly after that, I began working with boards in Central America. During my tenure at Hay, I was also invited to write a regular column ("The Boardroom") for BusinessWeek.com (now Bloomberg BusinessWeek.com), which has been a terrific experience. I left Hay in 2009 to start working on this book—and opened my own consulting practice, Board Advisor, based in New York.

I learn something new from every board that I work with. I have the privilege of working with capable, smart, extremely accomplished people on major issues impacting their companies, the people who work at those companies, and the shareholders who invest in them. Since I began working with boards in 1996, my goal has always been—and continues to be—to leverage the board so that it truly makes a positive difference for those companies. I believe great companies deserve great boards. And so do the CEOs who run those companies.

New York City   BEVERLY BEHAN
November, 2010

Introduction: Welcome to the Boardroom

Working with the Board of Directors is one of the most important components of any CEO's job—one that has changed dramatically in the past ten years. For most of the 1990s, the "imperial CEO" was the norm: CEOs selected their board members—often close friends—and board appointments were almost honorific. That changed in 2001 with the fall of Enron and the scandals at Tyco, WorldCom, Adelphia, and others, as well as the passage of the Sarbanes-Oxley Act and the NYSE and Nasdaq's introduction of new corporate governance rules designed to strengthen board independence from management. These changes were further amplified with the collapse of Lehman Brothers and Bear Stearns, followed by the debacles at AIG, General Motors, and Bank of America.

The CEO of today enters a very different boardroom landscape. Average CEO tenure in the United States is now five years or less. While some CEOs stay in office much longer, the press is awash with ugly stories of those who lasted half that time. Now under unprecedented scrutiny from the business media, boards no longer have any hesitation to "fire the coach" if things are going badly, or if directors feel in any way at risk from the CEO in terms of potential exposure or embarrassment. Indeed, in the thirteen years that I've been working with boards and CEOs, I've seen more CEOs terminated by their boards for "trust issues" than for "performance issues." A CEO whom the board trusts will nearly always be given much greater latitude to ride out performance downturns than one who has failed to earn that trust. For the latter, the first specter of a performance problem can be used as the basis for a walk down the plank.

The working relationship that you build with your board plays a significant role in earning their trust.

Over the past decade, the amount of time CEOs spend working with their boards, collectively and individually, has increased dramatically, to as much as 25 percent of their time, according to a study released in early 2010.[1] When I first saw that number, I asked the study's sponsor, Bill Johnson, Chairman and CEO of H.J. Heinz Company, if he actually devoted one quarter of his time to board-related issues. He not only confirmed that this mirrored his own experience, but he told me: "The percentage of time a CEO spends interacting with the board and individual directors may vary based on the tenure of the CEO. A relatively new CEO should be spending more time working with the board and establishing an effective working relationship with the directors than a CEO who is more long-tenured and has already built a strong relationship and a lot of credibility with the board. However, 25 percent of your time is roughly the right number, in my view. I'd go even further and say that if you're a new CEO, you have virtually no chance of being successful if you aren't spending at least 25 percent of your time on this."

Given the importance of this issue, it's hardly surprising that the majority of CEOs I've interviewed over the past five years have told me that the one thing they wish they knew more about before taking the corporate helm was how to work with a Board of Directors. Most CEOs step into their role with relatively limited boardroom experience, and this is particularly true for those who were promoted internally after a lengthy and successful career at the same company. Of course, you've presented time and again to your own board throughout your ascension; and during the last few years before your CEO appointment, you were probably in every meeting. But unless your board was prescient enough to encourage you to sit as a director of another public company, yours is the only corporate board you may ever have seen in action.

Even CEOs hired in from the outside, who may have worked with another board as an executive or even as CEO, have the benefit of only one or two additional boardroom data points. Moreover, executives typically learn their boardroom skills from watching their boss. But that may not be the optimal way to work with your board when you become CEO. This book offers different approaches CEOs have successfully used that are intended to help you raise your game beyond that of your predecessor—and build a much more effective board in the process.

Unless you started the company or took it through its initial public offering, you probably won't have the opportunity to build your board from scratch. You have to start with the hand you've been dealt in the boardroom—and I have seldom worked with a new CEO who didn't want to make some kind of change to the board.

Some CEOs want to say goodbye to one or more of the directors who have passed their sell-by date in terms of what they can offer the company and replace them with new blood, with skills and experience more relevant to the company's issues today. Others inherit a toxic director who is actively creating dysfunction and hostility in the boardroom. Still others are just plain frustrated with all the time they're spending with the board and the minimal value they're getting on any issues of importance.

The purpose of this book is threefold:

1. To help you establish a highly constructive working relationship with your board
2. To help you successfully address some of the dysfunction that may lie within the board you've inherited, while avoiding the kinds of political missteps that can jeopardize your job
3. To show you how to actually make your board a significant asset to you, your company, your shareholders and your executive team—something many boards are not.

Let's talk about the third objective for just a moment, because most CEOs tend to be satisfied if they achieve only the first one or two.

THE BOARDROOM: THE ULTIMATE TONE AT THE TOP

In 2004, I worked with the board of a mid cap company that had just spun off its largest business unit—and with it, half of its board and much of its executive team. This board was by no means ineffective: It had good practices relative to financial oversight and executive compensation, and its committees complied with all of the responsibilities enumerated in their charters. But it added almost no real value for the company. In fact, the directors had become stuck in bad practices that made the CEO and executive team dread working with the board.

Two years later, after some hard work, it was a different story. Meetings ended on time—some even finished early—and executives had their full time allotted on the agenda. Moreover, instead of just "presenting," the time they spent with the board focused on dialogue between the board and the executives. This was an actual meeting instead of a "presentation show." The checked-out, library-like atmosphere had become interactive, even vibrant. I asked an executive I had interviewed in 2004 what he thought of the board now, anticipating only a mild endorsement of the changes, given that he was a cynic by nature. Instead he told me, "This board is night and day from what we had before. They come into those meetings ready to roll—and they really work hard in there."

Three years after that, the executive had retired, and I spoke to other members of the CEO's senior team, some of whom had never worked with the pre-2005 board. Here's what they told me: "Working with our board is the best professional development experience I get in my job." "We were very keen on a particular recommendation earlier this year, and the board raised an issue that really made us stop and think. It caused us to change our course—and ultimately we took a different approach." "Because the board comes at the issues from so many different angles, it has caused me to really raise my game. If I present something to the board, they will challenge me. And I know that if I meet those challenges, I'm in good shape to present this on Wall Street or anywhere else. It gives me confidence."

My point in sharing this story is to show that dramatic change in a board is possible to achieve in only a couple of years—and that it is sustainable. Five years out, this board was even better and showed no signs of reverting to its 2004 doldrums. Later in the book, we'll talk about what that CEO did to affect this kind of dramatic change—and how you can do the same with your board.

I also share the story as a means of putting to you, as a Chief Executive Officer (and possibly Chairman of the Board as well, given that over half of U.S. public companies still combine these titles) some critical questions: What do your executives say about your board? Do they consider board meetings to be valuable experiences that they actually enjoy and learn from? Or are they necessary evils that most wish they could skip?

Nearly every CEO is concerned about the tone that his leadership sets at the top of the organization, but many fail to consider their Boards of Directors as part of that equation. They often self-identify with the management team rather than the board when, in fact, they are a member and often the leader of the board. In fact, your credibility as CEO suffers mightily if the tone in your boardroom differs dramatically from the tone you are trying to set in the rest of your company. One CEO put it this way: "How can I go to my people and tell them that we are committed to excellence, to be the best in the world—and then they come in to present to my board and see people who are checked out or asking off-the-wall questions? That reflects on me."

This book will outline the steps you need to take to change your board from mediocre (or worse) to a board that serves as a genuine asset for you, your senior executive team, your company, and your shareholders. Not only can it be done—it can be accomplished in two years and sustained for five years or more. Before we talk about transformation, however, let's discuss the lay of the land in most corporate boardrooms today.

SHIFTING CEO/BOARD DYNAMICS

While boards have become more independent and more engaged over the past decade, they have not become high-performing. Moreover, these are the views of directors, themselves. In nearly every survey of board members ever released by the National Association of Corporate Directors only a small percentage of respondents rate the boards they serve on as "highly effective". In the, the 2009 Public Company Governance Survey of 623 respondents who work with or serve on boards (two-thirds of respondents were outside directors), for example, only 23 percent rated their boards as "highly effective."[2] CEOs are hardly more generous: If you ask most top executives how many of their board members they view as highly effective—which Heidrick & Struggles partners Keith Meyer and Robert Rollo did in 2008—they will typically tell you that they have two or three "stars" but see the rest of their directors, and the board as a whole, as relatively ineffective.[3]

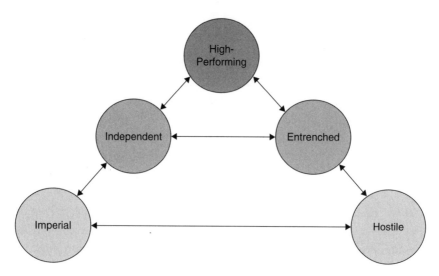

Figure I.1   Shifting Board/CEO Dynamics

Many people shake their head at these results, pointing to all of the changes that have swept through boardrooms in the past decade—changes that mandated greater director independence and expensive financial reporting requirements, among other things. They say, "After all this, our boards still haven't improved very much." In fact, they have. We have moved beyond the era of the imperial CEO—and while some CEOs may wistfully pine for the return to those "good old days," they are long gone in most U.S. boardrooms. But we are a long way from excellence. And excellence in the boardroom should be what a CEO aspires to cultivate.

Figure I.1 outlines one way to think about the shifting board/CEO dynamics that we've seen over the past decade.

- **The Imperial mode** characterized most boardrooms in the 1990s and prior. The CEO ran the company, selected the board—often from among his friends and colleagues—and board members viewed their roles as largely honorific, which they were. Directors asked a few questions to get their names in the minutes, but issues of consequence were largely decided by the CEO, with relatively minimal dialogue with the board. Most CEOs had one or two trusted advisors among the directors whom they might call late at night if they really wanted some advice on a thorny issue. In the meetings, board members typically avoided areas of questioning that might make the CEO uncomfortable or defensive. Major disputes between the board and CEO typically led to a director's resignation rather than the CEO's dismissal. It was not uncommon for directors to serve on many boards—some high-profile U.S. directors sat on as many as ten public company boards in the 1990s. After all, the workload was minimal, and more board appointments denoted increased prestige.

- **The Independent mode** characterizes the majority of North American boards today. In the United States, this shift largely began in 2003, with structural changes occasioned by the adoption of new corporate governance rules by the New York Stock Exchange and the Nasdaq in response to scandals at Enron, WorldCom, and Tyco. The new rules required that the boards of listed companies have a majority of outside, independent directors and that the Audit, Compensation, and Nominating/Governance Committees be composed entirely of outside, independent directors. Moreover, the independent Nominating/Governance Committee was to assume responsibility for the recruitment and renomination of board members—shifting this mandate away from the CEO. In addition, boards were to regularly meet in executive session without the CEO or other members of management present. All of these structural changes were designed to beef up director independence and put the board in a greater check-and-balance role than typically existed in the Imperial regime. And they had impact: Independent boards do operate much differently than Imperial boards. Board members take their jobs as directors more seriously and are highly sensitive to potential criticism if they don't fulfill their duties. Most directors of an Independent board genuinely want to make a contribution to the company and point to the fact that boards are much more engaged today than they were a decade ago. The problem, as the National Association of Corporate Directors studies illustrate, is that boards are still falling well below what they, themselves, consider to be "highly effective."

- **The Entrenched mode** is essentially the Independent board gone awry. An Entrenched board has typically adopted all of the stock exchanges' governance requirements and other best practices to separate the board from management. That's the good news: The directors have moved beyond the lemming-like dynamic of the Imperial mode. The bad news is that they have adopted a mind-set that focuses on preserving their jobs as board members and the comfort of their current operating mode, which they value far more than making any real difference for the company and its stockholders. Directors are highly complacent, make little contribution of consequence, and are ruffled by any new approaches or demands that could threaten their position and comfortable boardroom working mode they've developed. On paper, these boards comply with a host of good-governance practices—just like Enron did in 2000, when *Chief Executive* named its board one of the country's five best. Directors readily point to a high score awarded in a structurally based governance review, such as those conducted by many board rating services, as proof positive that the board is "good," while the company's CEO and executives—and often directors themselves—are well aware how little value the board adds to the organization. Resistant to change and far happier with being comfortable than high-performing, the Entrenched board is particularly challenging for a new CEO frustrated with the board's clubby dynamics and marginal contribution. Independent boards and Entrenched boards look similar on paper; they both have adopted a host of best practices and other structural niceties. Neither is high-performing. The difference, however, lies in the mindset: The Independent board wants to be high-performing but hasn't yet found the right way to achieve this. The Entrenched board is perfectly happy with the way things are and highly resistant to meaningful change. Notably, it is possible to find Entrenched directors on an Independent board and vice versa, to the point that it is sometimes difficult to define the predominant mode in which the board operates.

- **The Hostile mode,** characterized by a polarization between the board and management, is a scenario that most CEOs dread. The CEO is typically guarded with the board, shares minimal information with them, and reacts defensively to their questions. On the other side, directors lack trust and confidence in the CEO.

They know that the information they are receiving is *de minimus* and spend much effort in board meetings probing and interrogating for further information—often in aggressive, even accusatory tones—trying to draw out what they are not being told. It is often not a question of whether, but merely when, they will fire the CEO; offline director discussions about timing and identifying a replacement are frequent. Most directors want to feel they have been fair before pulling the plug, especially if the CEO has been in harness only a short time. Concerns about "the devil we know versus the devil we don't" are often the reason they hold off, as they seek to gather more information about external and internal candidates. Having one director take on the mantle of interim CEO often is the solution when the situation finally becomes intolerable to one side or the other. Inheriting a board that has been operating in Hostile mode may at first seem like a blessing to a new CEO—the bar is so low in terms of their dealings with your predecessor, how can you possibly do anything but improve upon this? But if unchecked, the board may quickly revert to this negative pattern of operating simply because they are comfortable with it. This happened recently to a retailer that, after protracted board/CEO hostilities, finally received the CEO's resignation. A honeymoon period with a new CEO (hired from the outside) ensued for several months. But before the year was up, the board and new CEO had slipped into the familiar Hostile operating pattern.

THE HIGH-PERFORMING BOARD

What are characteristics of a board that's operating in a high-performing mode? Here are some:

a. When you ask the CEO and the executive team how the board adds value for the company, they can answer that question right away—positively—and give you at least three examples of how the board has made a difference in terms of challenging their thinking, offering useful perspectives, or helping them in other ways that have genuinely had impact on board-level decisions. If you ask this question and the CEO and executive team can't answer it, roll their eyes, or insist that the board adds value but can't give specific examples, you don't have a high-performing board.

b. When you ask individual board members—in confidence and candidly—how the board adds value for the company, they can answer the question and provide specifics. The specifics pertain to significant issues that validate that the board is spending its time on the most important issues impacting the company—and its shareholder value—such as strategy, succession planning, risk oversight, and financial oversight. If they struggle with the question or refer you to the governance policies on the company Web site, you don't have a high-performing board.

c. When you ask individual board members if the board can improve in any way, they are able to make at least two or three worthwhile suggestions to further enhance the board's performance. High-performing boards become that way by adopting a mantra of continuous improvement. They are always thinking about ways to be even better—that's what makes them so good. If a director can't answer that question, she is likely set in a complacent or entrenched mind-set. If the rest of the board mirrors this perspective, the board will be unable to achieve sustained high performance.

d. The board meetings are typically characterized by openness and vibrancy. Few people do their best work in a stale or stifled atmosphere, particularly if they are working together as a group, as boards must do. The tone in the boardroom should not differ dramatically from the climate that the CEO wants to set throughout the organization.

e. The company achieves good results—financially, operationally, and strategically. After all, you can develop the world's best board in terms of its composition, dynamics, how it focuses its time, and how it works with management—and it won't matter one bit if the company it oversees isn't financially sound and performing well. The academic studies trying to link governance to stock performance are largely inconclusive. Yet, no matter how you slice it, a great board should steer a company toward positive performance and value for shareholders. Ultimately, this is the way in which the board provides the greatest value to the CEO as well.

So, if your board isn't high-performing, or if you don't perceive it that way, you're not the exception—you're in the majority. The point of this book is to show you how to take your board from wherever it is—simple mediocrity or downright dysfunction—to a level of performance that you, your senior team, and your company's shareholders deserve, and to avoid some of the classic missteps along the way.

CHAPTER 1

BOARDROOM PRIORITIES FOR NEW CEOS

ONE OF THE MOST PROFOUND CHANGES in any new CEO's work life is that he reports not to a boss but to a board. And to successfully lead the company, he must establish a constructive working relationship with that board. There are six things that any new CEO should consider doing to get that working relationship off to a great start. The timing of these may vary, depending on whether your predecessor continues to serve as Chairman subsequent to your appointment as CEO.

In the United States, where the majority of public company boards continue to combine the roles of Chairman and CEO, it is common practice for the outgoing CEO to continue to serve as Chairman for a transitional period at the end of the succession process. This period is much shorter today—typically about a year—than it was a decade ago, and it often helps to smooth the leadership transition. If this is your scenario, it may feel as though your working relationship with the board truly begins only after your predecessor finally exits the boardroom. Indeed, there are certain steps that should probably be deferred until after that occurs. However, four things are worth addressing in your first six to twelve months, regardless. These are:

1. Get comfortable with governance issues
2. Meet individually with every member of your board
3. Establish the terms of your working relationship with your Presiding Director or Nonexecutive Chair
4. Review the annual CEO evaluation process that the board will use to assess your performance.

1. GET COMFORTABLE WITH GOVERNANCE ISSUES

Serving on the board of another public company is invaluable experience for any new CEO. If you have not had this opportunity, it will be even more important to spend time on governance at the outset of your tenure as CEO. If possible, it can be useful to undertake some of these items in the six- or twelve-month period *preceding* your appointment as CEO. Otherwise, be sure to put them on the agenda for your first six months.

Prestigious business schools and other organizations offer many fine courses on governance; those at Harvard, Wharton, and Stanford are among the best known. You can ask your corporate secretary to track down course information and agendas to decide if any of these would be worthwhile. Admittedly, it can be difficult for any CEO to make time to attend an outside training session—particularly in her first six months after appointment. Even if you are able to do so, some CEOs find that the classroom environment inhibits them from raising important but often sensitive questions. Others simply feel uncomfortable asking what they perceive to be a "dumb question" in a forum where other attendees may think, "He doesn't even know that—and he's the CEO of *that* company?"

An alternative approach—or a means of supplementing any governance course you have taken or plan to take—is to design your own governance tutorial. I first became involved in providing individual governance tutorials for incoming CEOs in 2001; they worked so well that I have recommended this approach many times since. The agenda for this session should be tailored to cover topics of greatest interest to you. For example, if you have been hearing about "Say on Pay" or the "SEC Proxy Access Rule" but are uncertain of their implications, they may be worthwhile topics. If you have gathered agendas for some of the director-education courses, you may want to review these and cherry-pick the topics of greatest appeal in designing your own tutorial.

The quality of discussion in a governance tutorial differs markedly from what typically occurs in a director education class. In one instance I was involved in, the incoming CEO was particularly concerned about his predecessor's decision to offer a board seat to the company's chief financial officer (CFO), who had been runner-up in the succession process. The outgoing CEO viewed the board seat as a consolation prize for the CFO and had convinced the Nominating/Governance

Committee to go along with the idea. However, the incoming CEO dreaded having his former rival at the board table. Fortunately, the board had not yet informed the CFO of the decision. In addition to providing perspectives to the incoming CEO on this issue, we were also able to provide him with some data on board practices across U.S. companies, which showed that comparatively few CFOs serve as directors on their own company's board, even though most attend board meetings. Thus armed, the incoming CEO addressed the issue that very afternoon—and was successful in changing his boss's mind.

It's one thing to ramp up your knowledge on governance issues, but quite another to keep it current. If none of the leading governance publications—*Directors & Boards, Agenda, Directorship*, or *Corporate Board Member*—have been regularly hitting your in-basket, it's time to take out a subscription or two. Get some copies and see which periodicals you prefer. This will enable you to keep abreast of current governance issues and keep pace with your board members, some of whom are surely reading these publications. Indeed, it is not uncommon for directors to raise the very issues highlighted in these magazines at board meetings. Reading them yourself is a way to keep in front of these issues—and enables you to even be proactive in addressing some of them with the board.

2. ONE-ON-ONE MEETINGS WITH YOUR BOARD MEMBERS

Often a new CEO will have met with board members individually in the final stages of the succession-planning process. Then, why schedule yet another round of meetings? Because the last round was essentially a series of job interviews, with you in the role of applicant—the board's final due diligence before confirming your selection as CEO. Now that you've taken the job, it's time to begin your new working relationship. As Heinz Chairman and CEO Bill Johnson explains, "This is a very different conversation than one-on-one meetings you may have had with them when they were deciding to name you as CEO. That was the seduction process; once you've become the CEO, you're into the marriage."

You should aim to get these meetings under way in the first month or two after your appointment and to complete them within the first year—six months, if possible. However, it's critical to take your time with this process rather than rushing through it. One new CEO of a telecommunications firm who received this advice scheduled thirty-minute back-to-back meetings with each of his directors the day after his first board meeting. The result was far from what he'd hoped: Instead of building rapport with the board members, his mechanistic approach alienated them. "He clearly had some item on his to-do list involving director meetings, and it felt to us like he just wanted to tick that item off the list as soon as possible," one director complained. "He wasn't interested in having a meaningful conversation with any of us. When it was over, everyone began thinking the same thing: If this is how he's dealing with the board, how is he treating the executives and the other people at the company? Before long, there were phone calls going around, with board members wondering aloud if we'd made the right choice in naming him CEO."

It's best to schedule these meetings as dinners, lunches, or weekend brunches, preferably in the directors' hometowns rather than your own. Not only will you demonstrate respect for your directors if you get on the plane, but you nearly always will learn more about them as people on their home turf. Moreover, you will likely have a much more open dialogue than you would meeting in your office or at a restaurant near company headquarters.

Keep the agenda fairly open, since the objective of each of these meetings is primarily for you and the director to get to know each other a little better. But don't limit the discussion entirely to social topics—at some point in the conversation, you should steer the dialogue toward your board relationship. Ask directors what they've enjoyed most about being on the board and what, if anything, has frustrated or concerned them. Share your objectives for the company, and ask for their perspectives on the challenges and opportunities they see ahead. What do they see as priorities over the next six, twelve, or eighteen months? Canvass their views on the board/management relationship: What has worked well in the past, and what, if anything, would they like to change going forward?

One new CEO who asked these questions learned that her predecessor had been intensely resented for his imperious style. A director described the board/management relationship to her as "a mushroom farm. He kept us in the dark and fed us—well, you know—what they use to fertilize mushrooms." To demonstrate that she wanted to work differently with the board (once her predecessor had stepped down as

Chairman), she moved the next few board meetings from the company's austere boardroom to a downstairs lunchroom. It was the start of a great CEO/board relationship.

3. BUILDING A RELATIONSHIP WITH YOUR LEAD DIRECTOR OR NONEXECUTIVE CHAIR

WHAT'S THE DIFFERENCE?

A word at the outset about terminology, as it is sometimes confusing:

- *Nonexecutive Chair*: An outside, independent director who chairs board meetings and executive sessions, playing a key role in setting the agenda for board meetings and in overseeing the premeeting materials that are sent out to directors. Like the Lead Director, this individual also plays a role in keeping a finger on the pulse of the board between meetings and acting as a nonexclusive liaison between the board and the CEO, often meeting regularly with the CEO between meetings. Nonexecutive Chairs also lead the annual meeting of stockholders and are sometimes asked to represent the company externally as well, at employee or industry events.

  Examples: Some familiar examples of Nonexecutive Chairs at U.S. companies include Citigroup Chairman Dick Parsons, Walt Disney Chairman John Pepper Jr., and Campbell's Soup Chairman Paul Charron.

  Prevalence: While more than one-third of S&P 500 companies now split the role of Chairman and CEO, less than a fifth have an independent, outside board member serving as Chairman—in other words, a true Nonexecutive Chair.[1]

  Note: Retired CEOs who are asked to serve as Chair for a transitional period at the end of a succession do *not* qualify as Nonexecutive Chairs, because they lack independence from management under the stock exchange rules. More than a few companies have been embarrassed at stockholders' meetings or in the press after inaccurately applying this term to their outgoing CEO while he is serving as Chairman.

- *Chair or Executive Chair*: This term refers to someone serving as Chairman of the Board who is not considered independent of management, such as the company's outgoing CEO. In merger situations, where one company's former CEO agrees to serve as Chairman of the combined company for a transitional period, he would also be called Chairman but would lack the independence to be termed a Nonexecutive Chair. The term *Executive Chair* is often applied in controlled company scenarios in which an individual who is not independent of management (either a family member or executive of the control group, such as a parent company, or sometimes a former founder) has been designated as Chairman with the intent that he will serve in that role for a period far beyond a short transition.

Examples: Some familiar examples of Executive Chairs at U.S. companies include Microsoft Chairman Bill Gates, Ford Chairman Bill Clay Ford Jr., and *New York Times* Chairman Arthur Sulzberger Jr.

Prevalence: Some 35 to 40 percent of the S&P 500 separate the roles of Chairman and CEO. Only 16 percent have Nonexecutive Chairs; the balance have Chairs who are not considered independent of management. Among the latter, all but five have designated a Lead Director.[1]

- *Lead Director*: An outside, independent board member who chairs executive sessions, debriefs with the CEO afterward to give her feedback about what is on the board's mind, and also regularly interacts with board members and the CEO between meetings. There is no practical difference between a Lead Director and a Presiding Director in terms of role or responsibilities—it is purely a matter of titling.

   Prevalence: Spencer Stuart notes that "the lead or presiding director role is now a fixture on most S&P 500 boards"—95 percent now have them.[2]

- *Executive Sessions*: Since 2003, the governance rules of the New York Stock Exchange and the Nasdaq have required that board members meet regularly in executive sessions, with no members of management present—including the CEO. Most U.S. boards hold executive sessions in conjunction with every board meeting, usually immediately after the meeting ends. Less common practice is to hold the executive session prior to the board meeting, using it to organize and focus the meeting on priority issues.

   Many boards have now developed another practice in conjunction with the executive session required under the stock exchange rules: a meeting between the board members and the CEO with no other members of management present. This allows the directors and CEO to discuss issues that might be uncomfortable to talk about candidly with the CEO's direct reports in the room. After that meeting, the CEO steps out so the board can hold its required executive session. It is the responsibility of the Lead Director, who chairs the executive session, to debrief the CEO on issues resulting from it.

WORKING WITH YOUR LEAD DIRECTOR

An effective Lead Director can be an enormously valuable boardroom asset to any CEO—especially a new CEO. Lead Directors typically enjoy their fellow directors' respect and have a good understanding of the board's dynamics and its perspectives on key issues. Effective Directors play a liaison role between board members, doing their best to keep a finger on the board's pulse—staying in touch with directors and the CEO between meetings and being available if a director wants to talk about something that's on his mind. As such, the Lead Director can serve as a new CEO's early-warning system: Without violating board member confidences, she can let you know whether the board has concerns, what they are, and how you might want to address them before they become problems. This type of intelligence has enabled new CEOs to understand and address situations that might otherwise have cost them their jobs.

Most Lead Directors are happy to serve in a mentorship role to a new CEO in working with the board. In your first year or two, countless questions will arise about how to handle a particular matter with the board or about whether and how to address an issue that is on your mind. If the former CEO is still the Chairman, he can often provide guidance, but the Lead Director may be another useful resource—and on certain issues, perhaps an even better one.

The Lead Director can also run interference for the CEO on thorny board issues, including those that may arise with the outgoing CEO serving as Chairman. In one instance where a new CEO had been at the helm for two years and his predecessor showed no signs of packing his bags as Chairman, it was the Lead Director who finally "called the question" with the rest of the board and stepped up to the awkward conversation with the Chairman. In another, the Lead Director suggested at the outset that the board adopt a practice of having three executive sessions at the end of board meetings until the end of the CEO transition: one with both the former CEO as Chairman and the new CEO in the room without other members of management; a second session with just the new CEO talking to the board without the Chairman present; and the final session entirely without management. The second executive session—introduced to enable the board to talk to the new CEO without his former boss at the table—would never have occurred without the Lead Director suggesting it. It proved invaluable for all parties.

Take the time at the outset to talk to your Lead Director regarding how you want to work with her. Ask about the working relationship with your predecessor: How often did they meet or communicate between board meetings? What does she feel worked well in their relationship, and what changes might make your working relationship even more productive?

It's a good idea to schedule a series of regular meetings or calls with your Lead Director in your first six months as CEO. Some new CEOs like to check in with their Lead Director every week or two; others feel that a meeting or call once a month is just fine. Often these are supplemented by unscheduled calls when you'd find it helpful to get her opinion on a particular issue, or she wants the same from you.

Discuss also how and when you want to debrief after the executive sessions. Some CEOs and Lead Directors meet immediately after the executive session ends. Others feel tired after a long day of board meetings and plan their debriefing as a call or short meeting the next morning or even a few days later.

Clarify your own goals for this working relationship, and underscore that you need your Lead Director to be entirely forthright in sharing with you any negative feedback that may emerge in executive sessions or between board meetings. It's one thing to say this and quite another to respond appropriately when she delivers these kinds of comments. If you wince, cringe, or become defensive, regardless of what you may have told your Lead Director at the outset, this will be the last piece of candid feedback you'll ever receive from her. If that happens, your early-warning system with the board will effectively be broken.

The Lead Director has a duty to respect the confidentiality of board member comments in executive sessions and other conversations. Resist the temptation to probe the identity of the board member who may have expressed a particular viewpoint, and avoid any scenarios that would put the Lead Director in an awkward position around issues of director confidentiality. Otherwise, the net result will likely be far less candor in comments shared with you in the future.

WORKING WITH YOUR NONEXECUTIVE CHAIR

If you have a Nonexecutive Chair rather than a Lead Director, your preliminary conversation with her should cover the same items you would explore with a Lead Director. However, you will need to have more in-depth discussions on working together to set board agendas and on managing the meetings, given that the running of board meetings is the Chair's responsibility. It's essential that the Chair understand the priority issues relative to each board agenda so she can bear this in mind in leading the meetings. For example, if there are three critical items on the agenda, an effective Chair will ensure that there is appropriate time to discuss those items, even if this requires cutting off board discussion on earlier items. In scheduling your working sessions with the Nonexecutive Chair, ensure that some time is planned for this type of board meeting preparation. You and the Chair should come into board meetings well-coordinated and aligned.

Some companies provide office space and administrative support for their Nonexecutive Chairs. If this is the practice at your company, it will help you coordinate your meeting time together, which is likely to be somewhat more frequent than a CEO would have with a Lead Director or even a Nonexecutive Chair who does not regularly work at company headquarters. Most Nonexecutive Chairs who spend time in the office often meet with members of the executive team while they are there, and it would be a mistake to interfere with this practice. However, it is useful to put some coordination in place with the Chair around those meetings—finding out who she would like to talk to, what the subjects will be, and so forth. Don't feel constrained to leave the decision making on these meetings entirely to the Chair, either. If you feel that it would be useful for one or more of your executives to debrief with the Chair so she becomes more conversant on a particular issue scheduled to be discussed at an upcoming board meeting, suggest this to her. Or if a particular executive could benefit from her guidance on a matter he is working on, make this recommendation. The Chair will probably be delighted to have your input, and the meetings them-selves may become more productive.

4. REVIEW THE ANNUAL CEO EVALUATION PROCESS

One of the biggest challenges of reporting to a board rather than a boss involves your annual performance evaluation as CEO. While the Lead Director or Chair may lead this process on behalf of the board, it is nonetheless a performance evaluation developed by a group rather than an individual. For this reason in particular, you need to take a look at this issue sooner rather than later in the months following your appointment as CEO.

Historically, CEO performance appraisals were fairly superficial. Over the past decade, however, the public outcry on executive compen-sation and the generally increased level of board engagement, has taken us to a point where nearly all boards now have some sort of annual evaluation process for their CEOs. These range in style from appraisal forms with enough goals and measures to make anyone dizzy, to a brief conversation about the financial results that will be plugged into the bonus-plan metrics. You will find it very illuminating to learn how the board intends to appraise your performance at the end of the year. It is something many CEOs don't ask about until that first year is over, and some are shocked by what they discover.

There are two different elements to consider in the design of a CEO evaluation:

Evaluation components: What are the key measures that will be used in the performance appraisal? Will it be limited solely to finan-cial metrics? Or will other measures be included, such as customer-satisfaction ratings, market share, or the achievement of specified milestones, such as entering a geographic region within a certain time or bringing a new product to market by year end? Most CEO perfor-mance appraisals include some sort of form that is completed by board members, offering their rating of the CEO's performance on a variety of dimensions. Reviewing this form may be eye-opening.

One CEO of a financial services company found that the form his board had been using—and was planning to use again for his perfor-mance review—included items that the directors could only speculate about such as, "The CEO is respected by the company employees" and, "The CEO has communicated the strategic vision throughout the organization." "It's not that these are things are unimportant in terms of my performance as CEO," he explained. "But the board meets only six times a year and has pretty minimal exposure to the people who work here other than the members of senior management. What are they going to use as their basis for answering these questions - an elevator conversation with a staff member on the way up to a board meeting?"

The truth is, directors are always forming impressions about your performance from every conversation and interaction relating to the company. That said, including questions in your performance review where the answers are largely speculative is inappropriate and unfair. By the same token, most CEOs feel there is a lot more to their job than just hitting the numbers and want their performance appraisal to include broader factors relative to their leadership—going beyond stock price, return on assets, or other measures that might translate into bonus money. Working with your directors to arrive at what those key factors should be—and how they should be measured—is a critical conversation and one that need not be complicated.

Evaluation process: There should be three parts to the CEO evaluation process: a beginning, middle, and end.

- **The beginning:** The beginning should occur in the fourth quarter of the year prior to the fiscal year at issue or the first quarter of the fiscal year itself. This is a discussion between the CEO and the board to clarify your key objectives and goals for the year as CEO. This discussion should also address the way in which each of these will factor into your performance evaluation at year's end. This is one of the most crucial conversations you will have with your board all year—and it is even more important for a new CEO. If there is any sort of misunderstanding between you and the board on company priorities, this is where it will surface— and far better to surface at this stage than when the year is nearly over and you learn the board is disappointed because you haven't focused on something they felt was critical.

  Probably the best way for you to go into this conversation is with a list of at least three and probably no more than seven things that you see as your most important objectives for the year. Once you have reached alignment on these priorities, you can discuss how the achievement of each will be measured when your performance is reviewed at year's end. It is not uncommon to begin this dialogue with your Lead Director or a few of the directors who serve on the Compensation Committee. However, you will also find it valuable to have a discussion with the full board to confirm your priority objectives once you have established them with the smaller group.

- **The middle:** New CEOs find it particularly valuable to have an informal mid-year performance discussion with the board. Again, a discussion with your Lead Director or Chair may precede a discussion with the full board. However, there should be a larger discussion scheduled as a session of *only* board members and the CEO at the end of the second quarter or beginning of the third. The goal of this discussion is simply to dust off those objectives that you set at the outset of the fiscal year and talk about how you feel you are doing in accomplishing them—and how the board feels you are doing. If another priority has arisen that may supersede one of the initial objectives, you need to raise this with the board and come to agreement on how to handle it.

  This conversation can serve to elicit any concerns or misunderstandings far before year's end, when they may otherwise come as a surprise at a point where there is little that you can do about them. It can also confirm the board's support if you feel that things have been going well. They may be particularly impressed with something you did and really thought nothing of. This is all useful feedback—and particularly helpful feedback as you forge your working relationship with the board as a new CEO.

- **The end:** The final phase generally begins in the fourth quarter of the fiscal year and continues into the first quarter of the following year. It is at this stage that whoever is leading the CEO evaluation process on behalf of the board will begin collecting appraisal feedback. This will typically consist of collecting data on financial and other performance measures, feedback from the board, and any other information that you have agreed will serve as a component of the performance appraisal, such as customer-satisfaction ratings, data relative to key strategy implementation milestones, etc.

  It is common practice for the CEO to provide the board with a written memo outlining his views on performance during the year, referencing the key objectives and discussing areas of achievement as well as any shortcomings. If this has been skipped in the past, it is something you may wish to raise with the board when you are discussing the assessment process. Directors often find it very helpful to receive the CEO's thoughts on his performance, particularly from a CEO in his early years of corporate leadership. Among other things, it lets them know where the board and CEO may be aligned or differ on performance issues.

The company's year-end financial results need to be confirmed by the Audit Committee before they can be used by the Compensation Committee to determine their implications on compensation for the CEO and other members of the executive team. It's important to recognize this and have patience with the board as this process unfolds.

Once all of the information necessary to be included in the performance evaluation has been collected by whoever is leading the process, she will prepare a written evaluation and meet with you one-on-one to discuss it. Typically, the Lead Director plays a leadership role in the annual CEO evaluation. However, sometimes a team of two or three board members—the Lead Director and the Chair of the Compensation Committee, for example—conduct the meeting.

Many CEOs like to discuss their evaluation with the entire board as well. One CEO who is a fan of this practice explained her reasons: "It's not that I don't trust the Presiding Director to give me the board's feedback—it's just that he is summarizing what everyone said, and you miss some of the nuances that can be important. When you talk to all of them together, you get it from the horse's mouth, so to speak. At least twice when I've done this, I've had important things come out of that meeting that never arose in the one-on-one performance discussion." If this is also your preference, make sure you ensure that this is included as part of your evaluation process.

TWO FINAL STEPS

All of the foregoing are steps that any new CEO should take in the first six to twelve months, regardless of whether the former CEO remains on the board as Chairman during that time. Here are two others that may be awkward if he is still running the board meetings but should be addressed within six months thereafter:

5. Setting board/management expectations; and
6. Discussing emergency CEO succession planning.

5. SETTING BOARD/MANAGEMENT EXPECTATIONS

Setting expectations is very different than setting objectives for your performance review. This exercise focuses on the board/management relationship and seeks to capture some of the essential elements that are fair for each party to expect from the other in working together. In developing a set of expectations consider some of these questions: As CEO, what do you expect from the board and the people who serve on it? How do you want to work together with them going forward? How do they add value for you and for your senior executive team in their work as board members? What they can and should the board expect from you and your senior management team?

This can also be a fruitful area of discussion in your one-on-one meetings with board members. Some of the questions you may wish to explore with them include: What are your expectations of me and my senior team? What do you need from us in order to fulfill your duties as a director? What do you think that management can and should be able to expect from the board? How do you want us to work together? What worked particularly well in terms of the board/CEO relationship when my predecessor was CEO? What changes, if any, would you like to see in the way that the board and management works together going forward?

Asking these sorts of questions forces board members to stand back and really think about the working relationship between the board and management—something they may rarely, if ever, have considered in the past. It also helps you understand how the directors want to work with you as CEO—and where they may value a different approach to that taken by your predecessor.

Whether you choose to gather director feedback as part of this process, or simply to create a set of expectations that reflect your own perceptions, developing an Expectations List and having a good discussion about it with your board can be a very useful exercise at the outset of your working relationship. An Expectations List that one new CEO developed is presented in box 1.1.

Box 1.1   Sample Expectations of Board and Management

Expectations of the Board

- Make it a point to learn about the company's business, and keep abreast of developments in our industry.
- Prepare for board and committee meetings, having read the pre-reading materials and considered some key questions for the discussion of agenda items.
- Draw on your experience and knowledge to provide the company with your very best thinking and perspective on the issues we are wrestling with.
- Get engaged in the board debates. Don't try to dominate the conversation, but saying nothing in meeting after meeting is not OK, either.
- Say what you have to say in the board meetings—don't wait for "the meeting after the meeting" to express your views.
- Offer contrary perspectives whenever appropriate, but express your views in a way that demonstrates respect for fellow directors, management, and anyone else who may be presenting to the board.
- Give 100 percent of your share of mind in board and committee meetings—don't spend time on your BlackBerry or reading a memo from some other company or running out to take cell-phone calls. Be fully present and engaged.
- Come to decisions on the agenda items—don't keep putting them off. Once the board makes a decision, support it even if you personally held a different view on the issue.
- Create a positive board culture where directors and management genuinely enjoy the time spent working together.

Board Expectations of Management

- Be entirely open and honest in running the company and in dealing with the board. If there is bad news, share it with the board—don't try to hide it.
- Run the company with the highest ethical standards, and deliver on the financial and operating results we have promised. If financial or operating results will differ markedly—in either a positive or negative way—let the board know as soon as possible and provide an explanation for the variance.
- Keep the board informed of any significant developments affecting the company. The board should never be the last to know or put in the embarrassing situation of seeing an item about the company in the newspaper before they hear about it from management.
- Use the board as a thought-partner and sounding board, drawing on directors' experience as a resource to management in decision making. Don't bring everything to the board fully baked and just ask, "Any questions?"
- Provide the board with pre-reading materials that give directors the necessary information for board decision making, framed in a way that can be readily understood.
- Give the board exposure to high-potential executives so as to better facilitate board discussions on succession planning and the company's talent pipeline.
- Create a corporate culture that is positive and energizing for the employees who work for the company—and take the same approach in your dealings with the board.

6. EMERGENCY CEO SUCCESSION PLANNING

Up to now, your board probably had a pretty good emergency CEO succession plan—particularly if you were an internal promotion rather than an outside hire into the role of CEO. *You* were the plan. As the time of the CEO transition approached, the board became more confident in your readiness to step in if your predecessor were hit by the proverbial bus. Moreover, if something had happened to you up to now, the former CEO serving as Chairman would have been the obvious solution. However, once the CEO transition is complete, there is no longer a plan.

Not only is this an issue that is undoubtedly on the minds of your board members, having the emergency CEO succession discussion with them enables you to open up a dialogue that you will find extremely useful. It will give you invaluable insights on how the board views the members of your executive team. Put this discussion item on the agenda for that meeting of *just* the CEO and the board within the first six months after your predecessor has left.

Chapter 6 discusses emergency CEO succession planning in detail. However, a hit-by-a-bus succession discussion led by a new CEO soon after taking the helm need not involve all of the elements in an emergency succession plan that you might put together later in your tenure. It is enough to simply start off the conversation by acknowledging that the recent leadership change warrants this discussion and put forward a proposal to the board for what you believe might be a workable plan if the bus came by tomorrow. Then open it up for discussion.

Consider the earlier example of the CEO whose rival, the CFO, nearly became a board member. Not only did that incoming CEO want the CFO out of the boardroom, he wanted him out of the company. But he believed that the CFO had many supporters at the board level and felt that his hands were tied. He put the topic of emergency CEO succession planning on the board agenda for a discussion with only himself and the board in the room. He recommended that a board member serve as interim CEO in a crisis. An inevitable discussion ensued about the CFO and his suitability as an emergency succession candidate.

Indeed, the CFO had a couple of supporters in the boardroom. However, the new CEO discovered that, in fact, many directors had become deeply disenchanted with the CFO during the succession process. Finally, one board member said, "I certainly wouldn't say he's your backup plan, so I agree with that. And quite frankly, I don't see him staying at the company for very much longer. What do you think? Do you really want this guy on your team?" The new CEO was taken aback and initially responded with some comments about trying to keep the team together and bringing the CFO into the fold. "Look, that's all really nice," another director responded. "But the truth is, I think this guy is a problem for you. I don't think you can trust him as one of your most important lieutenants in running this company. And just so you know, if you feel you need to put a package together for him, I support that. What do the rest of you think?" Before the CEO knew it, he had the board's endorsement to say goodbye to the CFO.

Admittedly, a windfall result like this doesn't happen every time. The discussion could have gone entirely the other way and confirmed the CEO's fears of strong board support for the CFO. Either way, though, it was sure to provide the CEO with useful intelligence that he would not have acquired otherwise.

In Summary

One of the most profound changes for any new CEO is having a board, rather than a boss, to report to. Building a constructive working relationship with that board begins in your first six months as CEO. If your predecessor continues to serve as Chairman for a transitional period, it may feel as if your board relationship truly begins only after he finally exits the boardroom. Nonetheless, there are four steps that you need to take in your first six to nine months, regardless of whether or not he continues to serve as a director. These include:

- **Getting comfortable with governance issues:** Starting to regularly read board-related trade publications, attending a course, or designing a private tutorial tailored to governance issues you're particularly interested in will help you become more conversant on governance-related topics.
- **Meeting individually with each of your directors:** A critical first step in the foundation of your working relationship as CEO and board member, the discussion should focus not only on simply getting to know each other, but also should include questions focused on the CEO/board relationship.

- **Establishing the terms of your working relationship with your Lead Director or Nonexecutive Chair:** An effective Lead Director or Nonexecutive Chair can be one of a new CEO's most valuable assets, letting you know about any performance concerns the board is expressing (before they become problems) and serving as a resource for you on a variety of board issues.
- **Reviewing the annual CEO evaluation process:** One of the most unique facets of a CEO's job, unlike that of any other executive, is that her evaluation is conducted by a group of people, namely the board, rather than a single individual. This factor alone requires greater communication around this process and management of it. Determine what components should be included in your annual performance review and the steps in the evaluation process.

Two additional steps, which may be uncomfortable to discuss with the board while your predecessor remains as Chairman, should be addressed shortly thereafter:

- **Setting board/management expectations:** Define what you expect from directors in your working relationship with them, and what the board can and should expect from you and your management team. It may be worthwhile to explore these expectations in your one-on-one director meetings before finalizing them.
- **Emergency CEO succession planning:** During the last stages of the succession plan, you were the emergency solution if something happened to your predecessor. As Chairman, he was the solution if something happened to you. Now that the leadership transition has been completed, this is an important topic for the board to address. Doing so will also provide you with valuable insights about how the board views the members of your executive team.

CHAPTER 2

STRATEGY—THE FIRST BIG TEST WITH YOUR BOARD

MANY BOARDS CONSIDER THE OVERSIGHT OF CORPORATE STRATEGY their most important governance responsibility. For the past two years, "strategic planning and oversight" has ranked first—by a wide margin—in national surveys of U.S. public company directors about their top priorities.[1] Despite its importance, few directors give their boards high marks in this area; in a 2009 survey, less than 20 percent rated their boards as "highly effective" on strategy issues.[2] As this study suggests, there is clearly room for improvement in how boards engage with the CEO and management on issues of strategic oversight.

One of the first critical tasks any new CEO must undertake is a review of corporate strategy with the board. This is true even in circumstances where a new CEO is an internal promotion with a mandate to continue implementing her predecessor's strategy. Any new CEO needs to put her own stamp upon the company's strategic direction—and make any required changes to the strategy, even if modest. In other circumstances—more typical when a new CEO has been hired from outside—he may be asked to develop a dramatically different strategy for the company, or perhaps even create a strategy if none really existed in the past. Typically, incumbent CEOs engage with their boards on strategy issues in depth at least once a year, often at a strategy off-site that involves either reviewing the current strategy and discussing progress and modifications to it, or developing a new strategic direction for the company.

This strategy review is typically a defining moment of the board and CEO relationship. Regardless of what the CEO has said about wanting to engage the board members—valuing their input, seeking their counsel—the rubber meets the road on the issue of strategy. Directors will then see if the CEO truly leverages their capabilities on this critical issue or sees the board as a rubber stamp.

I vividly recall the disappointment of one board member who had strongly supported an internal candidate's promotion to CEO: "Three months in, he's supposed to be laying out his strategic plan in a board meeting," the director said. "He schedules this for only two hours, presents a bunch of slides, and then says, 'OK, here's what I'm doing. Any questions?' And when we start to ask questions, he gets defensive. Let me tell you, when the board walked out of that meeting, this guy's honeymoon was over."

In an interview for BusinessWeek.com, Kimberly-Clark Chairman and CEO Tom Falk told me of a similar experience. Shortly after becoming CEO, Tom began working on corporate strategy: He used first-class strategy consultants, spent weeks working with his executive team to ensure he had analyzed all of the key issues, made a firm decision, and presented the finished package to his board in what he described as "graphs, charts—a PowerPoint festival." When he finished the presentation, Falk recalled, the directors told him that they agreed entirely with his strategic analysis and his recommendations—and then they said, "But don't ever do that to us again!" The board insisted on being far more engaged in future strategic issues rather than simply serving as an audience for canned presentations from the CEO.

Herein lies a classic mistake many CEOs—particularly those new to the job—make in working with their boards on strategy. Recognizing that strategy is their first big test with the board, new CEOs aim to come to the board with the strategy nailed, to impress the directors with all of their careful analysis, innovative alternatives, and well-considered recommendations. They believe that this is a way of earning the board's confidence in their leadership, and it certainly beats walking into the boardroom with weak analysis, few ideas, and an eagerness to hand over the problem of strategic planning to the board members. There is, however, a middle ground that not only yields a more favorable response from the board, but it can result in a more effective strategy and genuine board support for that strategy.

THE CEO "OWNS" THE STRATEGY

Let me address at the outset a nagging question that often arises on the issue of strategy: *The choice of strategy for a company is the choice of the CEO, not the choice of the board.* Simply put, the CEO and her executive team run the company and know it better than any of the outside board members, regardless of their business savvy, knowledge of the industry and even of the company. The CEO and the executive team work at the company day in and day out; it is the primary focus of their work life.

Board members, by contrast, have a tangential relationship to the company. They meet several times a year, do their best to understand the critical issues facing the company and to keep abreast of what's going on in the industry and the economic environment. Most genuinely care about the company's success and want to make a positive contribution to that success. But by the very nature of their roles as outside directors, they have day jobs or, at the least, other commitments. The share of mind that they can contribute to the company is limited; it will never come close to that which the CEO and other executives can give to the company's business. Therein, in fact, lies their value: Outside directors can stand back and see the forest despite the trees. They can offer a range of different perspectives on strategic issues that management may have missed or failed to think through. But they neither can, nor should be, developing the company's strategy.

Moreover, it is the CEO and management who are responsible for strategic implementation, so it is essential that they feel a strong sense of ownership for that strategy. The dynamics are entirely different—and not in a good way—when the CEO and senior team are asked to implement what is essentially the board's strategy; they feel no sense of ownership and commitment. The same dynamic occurs when a new CEO is asked to implement his predecessor's strategy, which is the reason why even a new CEO who has been essentially tasked to stay the course needs to conduct a review to affirm the strategic direction, take personal ownership through that process, and make necessary modifications to the strategy and its implementation plan.

But directors play a critical role: While it is the CEO who develops and owns the strategy, the board ultimately controls that strategy through its power to hire and fire the CEO. Any board that feels the CEO is off base in terms of strategic direction can, first, voice those concerns and recommend changes; and, second, terminate the CEO's leadership of the company if the strategic course remains unacceptable. For this reason, among others, the CEO needs to ensure that the board is genuinely aligned with the corporate strategy and fully supportive of it. This is more readily accomplished by a CEO who ensures that the board fully understands the reasons for her strategic choices and becomes constructively engaged in the strategic dialogue.

"DON'T WORRY, I'LL SMOKE IT THROUGH"

CEOs who present a completed strategy and watch it pass in the board meeting with minimal questions typically declare victory—but often suffer dire consequences later on. A CEO with whom I worked years ago did exactly this on a game-changing strategy he'd spent several months developing. Having worked with his board in the past, I expressed reservations when he told me that his plan for presenting the new strategy involved a presentation, by him and his strategy consultant, as a short agenda item at an upcoming board meeting. He replied, "They know it's coming, so it won't be a surprise. Don't worry, I'll smoke it through." And he did. The board asked few questions and gave its blessing.

But problems emerged at the next board meeting. The CEO sought board approval for the sale of two lines of business—one of them something of a sacred cow—that he deemed inconsistent with the strategy. The board pushed back strongly, and he found himself having to come back with further analysis and more information before they would green-light his proposals. At subsequent meetings, he encountered similar pushback: The CEO was seeking approval on certain investments required to move ahead with the new strategy and, again, to use his description, the board became "mired in details." The CEO left the meetings in frustration. "They just don't get it," he complained in the months that followed. Of course they didn't get it: He had spent almost no time securing their understanding or their genuine buy-in.

With every meeting, frustrations intensified on both sides. The CEO became more guarded; directors' questions were increasingly pointed. Finally, the CEO's closest ally on the board called him with startling news: The CEO was on shaky ground and needed to do something about it if he wanted to keep his job. The board questioned the sanity of his strategy—and his ability to execute it—and it didn't help that company performance had declined over the preceding six months. Board members had begun discussing possible outside recruits to replace him.

In this case, the CEO was smart enough to recognize how he'd gotten into this mess—and what he needed to do to get out, which was to engage the board on strategy in a way that he should have done in the first place. Not only did he save his job and put his relationship with the board back on solid ground, but this engagement kicked off a successful tenure as CEO that otherwise would have been quite brief. He recently retired after six years at the helm—and is about to join his first corporate board as an outside director.

BOARD MEMBERS WANT TO MAKE A CONTRIBUTION ON STRATEGY—AND MANY CAN

Engaging the board effectively in strategy review and development pays other dividends as well. Ask directors where they would like to make a contribution to the companies on whose boards they serve, and most will explain that they'd like to play a greater role in strategy. They are often frustrated because they feel the CEO under-leverages their experience and capabilities in this important area. Indeed, there is often a wealth of relevant experience and good strategic capability sitting around the board table that is largely untapped—and it never will be tapped as long as the CEO follows the pattern of presenting strategy to the board as a finished work.

The value of engaging the board as a thought-partner on strategy varies with the composition of your board and the effort expended to educate directors about the company, its industry, its operating environment (including competitors, consumer trends, legislative implications, investor profile, etc.), and other factors with significant strategic implications. Obviously, if you lack industry experience at your board table and/or corporate leadership experience—or that which you have is outdated—the board's contribution to strategic issues will be far less than if you have a strong portfolio of skills and experience to draw on.

Recently, I chaired a panel on "The Role of the Board in Corporate Strategy" at a conference of the National Association of Corporate Directors. One of the panelists argued that Sarbanes-Oxley and the recent focus on director independence have compromised the board's ability to engage in the type of worthwhile strategy discussions that would be possible with more inside and related directors at the table, individuals who would bring a greater understanding of the company and its business. He may not be wrong, but that pendulum is unlikely to swing back anytime soon. In the meantime, it would be a shame if suboptimal board composition were used as a rationale to continue to ignore those capabilities that *are* resident in the boardroom and fail to derive value from them.

WHY MOST CEOs ARE RELUCTANT TO ENGAGE THEIR BOARDS IN MEANINGFUL STRATEGY DISCUSSIONS

There are several reasons that CEOs tend to default to the "I'll smoke it through" approach when it comes to engaging their board on strategy:

a. *Losing control of the strategy decision.* The major reason that CEOs tend to limit their board's engagement on strategic issues is that they fear losing control of the strategy decision. Having opened the door to engage the board in strategy discussions, they worry that the board will hijack the process, leaving them as the implementer, rather than the owner of arguably their single most important decision as the company's chief executive.

In fact, this is an easy concern to overcome. It begins with the CEO, at the outset, having a conversation with the board about the respective roles of the board and the CEO in the strategy process. Get the board's confirmation that the choice of corporate strategy lies with the CEO, for all the sound and practical reasons outlined above. But recognize, in that discussion, that the board ultimately controls the strategy through its ability to hire and fire the CEO. Note that it is important to ensure directors' full understanding of, and alignment behind, the strategy; this is the very reason why you want to bring them into the discussions for a meaningful dialogue rather than simply presenting the strategy as a fait accompli. Point out that it is your intent to use the board as a thought-partner on strategy issues, even though you will enter those discussions with a clear and well-considered point of view. Their input, however much appreciated, may or may not be reflected in your ultimate recommendation.

I have yet to see a board that failed to play by these kinds of rules on strategy once the CEO outlined them. Most are delighted to have an opportunity to become more engaged in strategy review and development. They readily respect the boundaries the CEO lays down—and the reasons for them. As one board member explained, "I can live with almost any decision about the growth strategy for this company, unless it is something completely off the wall. But I have real trouble when a decision is reached and I haven't been given an opportunity for any input. If you don't accept my point of view, that's fine. But if you don't even give me a reasonable chance to express it, I have a problem with that. Among other things, it shows a lack of respect."

b. *Misperceptions of board expectations.* As discussed earlier, new CEOs in particular often believe that the board expects them to come into the strategy discussion with all dimensions of the new strategy finalized. In fact, bringing the board into the process sooner and using them as a sounding board on strategic issues typically receives a far more favorable response.

One director of a midcap company in the Midwest currently in the last phases of a CEO succession process explained: "One of the things our current CEO does very well is that he comes to the board with the strategy not completely baked. He's not asking the board to make the strategy decision or come up with the alternatives; he's thought it all through very comprehensively, and he has his point of view. Instead, he uses us as a sounding board at different stages as he develops his strategic thinking. It takes a lot of confidence for a CEO to do this with a board, but I think there are real benefits to this approach: Not only do we better understand the issues he's grappling with—it gives him the benefit of our advice and perspectives. I really hope the new CEO will have the confidence to tackle strategy with us in the same way."

The CEO in this instance also found value in the approach he'd developed. When he was asked how his board added value for him as CEO, he replied without hesitation: "Strategy is the area where they've really made a contribution. They bring in different perspectives and really challenge our thinking—but in a very constructive and respectful way. We have changed and refined some of our decisions on strategy because of their input, and it's caused us to make better choices—and avoid some missteps."

c. *Doubts that the board can make a contribution.* Another reason many CEOs are reluctant to bring their board under the tent on strategy is that they don't believe their board members have sufficient knowledge of their business to contribute to strategy discussions. One CEO put it this way: "Only one of my directors has any background in this industry. Even if I take the time to get the board involved in some type of strategy exercise, they're not going to add much to these conversations. They may even take us off track. Once I get a board with the right people on it, that will be the time to draw on the board's expertise relative to strategy issues, because then the board will be made up of people who can really contribute."

Strengthening your board by adding new directors who bring relevant skills and experience will certainly enable the board to make an even greater contribution on strategy discussions. However, it is hardly practical for a CEO—particularly a new CEO—to seek to completely overhaul the board's makeup in advance of the strategy review, typically scheduled within the CEO's first year, often in the first six months.

Even if you don't have the dream team around your board table, does it make sense to engage them on strategy? Actually, it may be even more critical to do so if you sense that they lack knowledge and a strong understanding of your business. After all, they are going to be evaluating your performance as CEO; they are going to be approving the funds, financing arrangements, and other resources you will need to move forward in implementing your strategy. They are going to be overseeing your financial and operating performance—and they need to fully comprehend how the strategy you are executing should translate into performance results. If they don't understand these things, waiting until there's a problem to explain them can be disastrous. Moreover, if directors have a fundamental misunderstanding of some of the critical aspects of your business, you need to correct that right away.

IS THE BOARD AT THE END OF THE STRATEGY LINE—OR THE FRONT?

When embarking on a strategy exercise—be it a comprehensive review of the current strategy or the development of a new plan—the CEO usually begins by working intensely with her executive team and often outside strategy consultants. Much time—and often sizeable

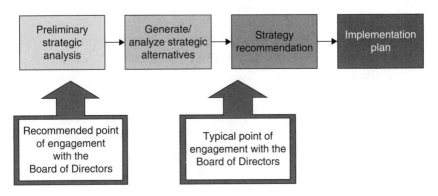

Figure 2.1   Basic Strategy Model

professional fees—is devoted to this exercise, with many late nights along the way. Finally, the strategy plan is pulled together and a polished presentation prepared, at which point the CEO—accompanied by her top lieutenants and occasionally the outside consultants—unveils it to the board. This could be done at a board offsite (where the senior management team and the board schedule a weekend away from company headquarters to focus on strategic issues) or at a regular board meeting.

By this time, however, the CEO and the executive team are heavily invested in the strategy recommendations they've developed. When presenting them to the board, they're typically looking for a pat on the back rather than substantive input. Of course, they expect and will tolerate some tire-kicking as part of the board's fulfillment of its responsibilities to shareholders. However, from the CEO's perspective, the worst possible outcome from this meeting is for the board to reject the plan and send management back to the drawing board. At this stage, company executives are signed up for the program and champing at the bit to move ahead. The CEO, then, is looking to defend the senior team's strategy, not reshape it. Above all, the CEO is aiming to avoid the board derailing the whole thing.

Consider a different approach—one that places the board of directors at the front of the line on strategy rather than at the end. To illustrate the typical model, let's use a simple graphic (see figure 2.1) that denotes four stages in the development of corporate strategy:

   a. **Preliminary analysis.** The standard analysis of strengths, weaknesses, opportunities, and threats, incorporating factors relative to the company's operating environment, including economic, competitive, industry, and (if applicable) regulatory/political factors.

b. **Generation and analysis of strategic alternatives.** Based on the preliminary analysis, a series of alternative strategic approaches will be generated. Each needs to be fleshed out and considered from a variety of standpoints, including required resource allocation/investment, key risks, synergies with existing business(es), anticipated return and over what reasonable period, management capabilities, barriers to entry/exit, competitive response, and so forth.

c. **Strategy recommendation.** The recommended strategy for the company either to embark upon or to maintain.

d. **Implementation plan.** A detailed plan for the implementation of the strategy, including timelines, investment requirements and anticipated returns, leadership/staffing for key roles, infrastructure issues (e.g., the need for a partner or for expansion of facilities), milestones, and so forth.

What if at the first stage the CEO were to engage the directors by gathering their views on the factors that go into the preliminary strategic analysis? For example: What do they see as the company's strengths relative to competitors? Who do they consider the key competitors? What changes in the industry do they feel present the company's greatest threats or opportunities? This is not to suggest that the executive team should turn over to the board the task of conducting the preliminary strategic analysis. The purpose of this dialogue is to enable the CEO to make sure that the board and management are aligned on all of the key issues that will form the underpinnings of the strategic alternatives and, ultimately, the strategic recommendations. There are three reasons for this:

- If there are significant differences between management and the board on any key strategic issues, it's far better for the CEO to identify these at the outset. They will come up sooner or later— either at the time the board and CEO are engaging on strategic alternatives/recommendations, or after the CEO is already heading down the path of execution.

- This process can help the CEO to immediately recognize areas in which the board may require more information or education about the business, the industry, or specific issues facing the company that factor into strategy decisions. These can then be addressed through presentations prior to the strategy offsite, providing pre-reading materials for the offsite, or in sessions at the offsite itself.

- Board members may, in fact, raise some issues that the management team hadn't considered. Far better to get that input at the outset, so that it can be factored into your own analysis, than have it trip you up during the big strategy presentation.

When the CEO is an outside hire new to the organization, these insights can be even more important because he lacks a veteran executive's institutional memory. However, this process can make even internally promoted CEOs aware of matters to which they were never privy in their prior roles. One new CEO who took this approach learned that a strategy he was seriously contemplating had been advocated by the CEO prior to his predecessor—and had been shot down by the board. He eventually recommended revisiting this strategy—but now knew enough to highlight key differences in consumer buying practices and technology that had developed in the past five years, making the strategy more attractive at this stage. He secured the board's support.

PRACTICAL EXAMPLES

STRATEGY AND THE POLARIZED BOARD

A new CEO I worked with recently came into his role from an executive position in another company. Within three months, he discovered that his board was polarized on a key strategy issue: Some advocated the direction he explicitly said, upon his hiring, he wanted to move toward; others strongly opposed this view. One of the opponents noted: "I thought you were the right guy for the job, so I supported your hiring as CEO. I figured that in time, you'd come around on where this company needs to be going."

The new CEO planned a board offsite to get this issue resolved—preferably in the way he wanted—and began working with his executive team and outside strategy consultants to prepare. At the same time, however, he asked me to interview each of the board members to solicit their views on the very issues that he, his team, and his consultants were factoring into their preliminary analysis. (Note: In this instance, the board interviews went beyond purely issues of strategy and included how the board wanted to work differently with the new CEO than they had with his predecessor.)

The CEO found the results of the directors' feedback extremely enlightening. Directors knew surprisingly little about two critical issues facing the company, and about their implications. He learned that two directors who strongly advocated the alternate course of action came to their position years earlier and had ignored recent changes in the economy and regulatory environment. Several board members also raised ideas and made points that the CEO hadn't thought of. Others pointed out risks and challenges that they were anxious to see addressed.

The feedback was summarized for the CEO in a way that enabled him to factor it into the preliminary analysis on which he, his executive team, and his consultants were working. It was also used in the design of the offsite itself. Speakers were arranged to address the two critical areas in which the board needed more information. In their pre-reading, directors received a summary of the key themes from the board interviews, enabling them to immediately understand areas of alignment and focus on points of contention. Exercises were developed to help the board and management work through the contentious issues.

On the final morning of the offsite, the CEO asked the board for consensus to develop a strategy and implementation plan in his recommended direction. Until then, half the board had supported a different direction. The board member who was the strongest advocate of the contrary strategy was the first to respond: He said that he had learned more about several important issues from the presentations, recognized the underlying reasons that others supported the CEO's viewpoint, and appreciated the need for consensus. He had changed his mind, he said, and endorsed the CEO's proposal.

STRATEGY AND THE "EXPERT" BOARD

Another new CEO joined a company whose board included four sitting CEOs who were joint venture partners in ownership of the company itself. Despite its unusual structure, this board had functioned quite well for nearly a decade. But the time had come to radically explore strategic options, and the new CEO was tasked with both developing a new strategy and executing it.

In contrast to our last example, this board had directors who knew almost as much about the business as did the CEO. They also had strongly different viewpoints on strategy—so much so that many feared it would be impossible to bring them into alignment on any direction going forward.

Through a similar set of interviews conducted with each member of the board and the executive team, it became clear that what was most needed was a forum to air and debate the different perspectives. Those board members who were sitting CEOs with ownership interests felt they had a lot to contribute to the strategy discussion—and they wanted to be heard. Board members who came from outside the industry desired the benefit of their views. The new CEO immediately recognized that while the board had clearly tasked him with developing a strategy, he could hardly revert to the typical point of engagement as referenced in Figure 2.1. Presenting this board with strategic recommendations and asking, "Any questions?" would be tantamount to releasing the lions in the Coliseum.

Wisely, the new CEO presented his board with two models of how he might work with the directors on strategy, which included timelines and a description of each stage of the strategy process and the board's role at that stage. The first was a fairly straightforward model—basically the typical point of engagement in Figure 2.1 with some tweaking. This alternative offered an accelerated timeline to meet directors' concerns that, "We need to get on this strategy thing right away." The second involved an expanded timeline reflecting the recommended point of engagement in Figure 2.1. It began with an offsite focused on the preliminary analysis, used the offsite conclusions as the basis for generating alternatives for discussion at the board meeting (two months later), and culminated in a final recommendation at the subsequent board meeting. Although the second model involved a six-month time horizon—twice as long as the other timeline—the board unanimously supported it. I last checked in with this CEO midway through the process, which he characterized as going extremely well.

Garbage In, Garbage Out

Earlier in this chapter, I acknowledged some CEOs' complaints that their boards lack sufficient knowledge of the business to engage effectively in strategic discussions. While changing the composition of the board—and adding directors with more relevant backgrounds—is part of the solution to this problem, another factor often gets in the way: the quality of information that board members receive about the company. If your predecessor fed the board a steady diet of financial information and almost nothing relating to the factors that will underlie your strategic analysis—industry trends, competitive landscape, technology change, regulatory/political environment—how can you expect the board to engage in meaningful strategy discussions?

Late last year, I received a call from the Chair of a Philadelphia-based educational organization; she lamented how "useless" her Board of Trustees was: "They don't know anything about how this organization works—how we actually make our money and what's going on with our donors that's caused everything to go sideways for us recently." I asked her what kind of orientation program directors received. "Oh, we don't do anything like that," she replied. "People don't have time for it. They just show up at the board meetings." Then I asked about the information board members received—what was in their board packages? "Not much, really. People don't have time to read that stuff. I just throw in some information about new programs, new faculty—and of course we look at the financials and how we're doing against our budget. That's most of it." "Well, you're the Chairman of this board," I reminded her. "It's up to you to educate your trustees about your organization in a way that would enable them to engage in strategic discussions. Yes, you may need some new people at your board table with backgrounds in education—which you don't have now—but that doesn't absolve you from the responsibility to educate the trustees you do have in a meaningful way."

If you're a new CEO and your predecessor abdicated his responsibilities in the same way that this Chair did hers, it means you have some work ahead of you to get your board members up to speed before you engage with them on strategy. Conducting interviews with the board—through the process described earlier—is one way to bring to the surface any "gaps" in their understanding of key issues and ensure that they're addressed. But I'd urge you to go even further. Ask yourself: If you were sitting on the other side of your board table, what kind of information would help you to better understand the business—without getting into a level of detail that would be described as micromanagement? Nearly every board with which I've worked in the past five years has told me that it would prefer more information on industry trends, competitors, key customers/suppliers, and new technology.

Be selective. If your board has been wandering for years in an information desert on some of these issues, don't suddenly produce a fire hose. Invest the time in having the information packaged in a way that directors will find easy to follow and understand. If you must send them lengthy reports of fifty or one hundred pages, include executive summaries. The reason to provide this material is not for show—it's to shore up the board's understanding of important issues that may impact your company's strategic choices. There is no point sending it to your directors if it fails to achieve this purpose.

Getting the Board out of the Boardroom

When was the last time your directors went on a site visit? Where have they visited in the past? I'm a huge fan of site visits. Not only do they typically earn rave reviews from employees who get a chance to interact with board members, but they provide directors with the hands-on experience of seeing facilities, customers, and new geographies in which the company does business—and in a way that profoundly impacts their level of understanding. The company's business comes to life for them in a way that no boardroom experience can replicate. Some of the more interesting practices that I've run across recently:

- Carol Stephenson, a director new to the board of General Motors, told me about her first board meeting. The night before, the directors met at GM's design facility, where executives took the directors through all of the steps and stages in product design, from the blank sheet of paper to the production line. The next day, directors were taken to the track, and the new models were brought out, including the Volt. Board members drove each of the vehicles on both a performance and city track. In the passenger and rear seats were members of the product team, who answered questions directors raised as they drove: Who were the primary consumers for this vehicle and in which geographies? Who were the major competitors, and what were GM's advantages and disadvantages relative to competitive offerings? "When I finished driving those cars," Stephenson concluded, "I understood those products better and in a far more fundamental way than hours of PowerPoint could have accomplished."

- Norm Augustine, the former Chairman and CEO of Lockheed Martin, who served as Presiding Director of Procter & Gamble, described a practice P&G adopted to give its board members a better feel for customers in distant geographies. When the board visited a country in Southeast Asia, for example, the P&G team arranged for small groups of directors to visit family homes at all levels of the economy, from poor families with dirt floors to those of higher incomes. The P&G directors observed how the families used P&G's products in their homes. Augustine described one of his insights from this experience: "The home I visited had a concrete floor, and this family didn't have much money. So I was surprised to see that they were using small packets of detergent, rather than the large, economy size. They explained that they didn't have a vehicle and had to walk several miles to the store where they purchased detergent. The economy size was too heavy to carry back home."

- Tom Falk, Chairman and CEO of Kimberly-Clark, began taking his board on annual visits to major customers such as Wal-Mart, Costco, and Target. He told me about his rationale for this practice: "The more the board knows about the business, the better the contribution they can make, particularly in discussions of corporate strategy. That's why every year we take the board to spend a day with one of our major customers. We have the board meet with our customer's senior leadership and discuss a variety of issues that can really help further their understanding of our business and the viewpoints of key people we do business with."

- Glenn Lyon, Chairman and CEO of athletic shoe retailer The Finish Line, implemented a new program in which board members join management teams on store visits at least one day each year. Directors can select which of the monthly store visits they want to participate in, giving them the option of seeing stores in different regions while accompanied by teams of senior executives who can answer their questions and point out new features of store redesign, displays, and so forth. The program also enables Finish Line's board members to spend some time one-on-one with members of Glenn's executive team outside of the boardroom.

If you're a new CEO, you may lack time to do much in the way of board site visits prior to your first strategy review with the board, but it's worth considering. Some companies combine a site visit to a facility along with a board offsite, although doing so may require a trade-off of time spent in strategy discussions. This may not be a compromise worth making, given the importance of your first strategy review as an incoming CEO. But even if it becomes impractical, you may nonetheless want to consider adopting some site-visit practices (along the lines of those outlined above) over the course of the next year. If you can pull it off—particularly if it is something your predecessor never tried—it is a subtle way to underscore to your directors that you expect them to learn about, understand, and keep abreast of what's going on in your business.

STRATEGY IMPLEMENTATION: UPDATES AND MEASURES

So much emphasis is typically placed on analyzing and deciding on the recommended strategy that strategic implementation, the very last phase of the process, often becomes an afterthought. However, this is a critical issue, particularly in terms of the board. The elegance of the strategy—and all of the brilliant analysis that went into it—pales quickly if that strategy cannot be effectively implemented to achieve the anticipated results. The board views "oversight of strategy implementation" as one of its key responsibilities and will want regular updates on your progress in executing the strategic plan. Key milestones or other measures of your success in strategy execution may also be incorporated into your annual performance appraisal, even if these do not directly translate into bonus money.

The final strategy recommendation should be accompanied by, or quickly followed up with, a relatively detailed implementation plan that outlines timelines and milestones as well as required investment, resources, and leadership assignments relative to new strategic initiatives. Without a comprehensive plan for execution, some boards refuse to sign off on a strategy recommendation, even when strategy discussions have addressed many of the implementation factors. They want to see it all laid out.

One of the chief complaints I hear from board members is that they receive only sparse updates on the implementation of the company's strategy. As one director described it: "We spent a lot of time as a board working with the CEO and her team on strategy issues. There was one issue in particular that caused everyone a lot of concern. Finally, we endorsed a strategic direction for the company that she wanted to pursue and approved a bunch of money that management said they needed to start the ball rolling. But since that time, we haven't heard very much about how they're doing in terms of putting this new strategy into place—or whether it seems to be working. It's too early for this to translate into financial results, but it's not too early to get some kind of update about their progress. I'm disappointed that we never seem to talk about this."

Using the implementation plan as a road map, you can determine when you will be in a position to provide the board with meaningful updates on your progress. In some cases, you will have an update for the board at the very next meeting—and at every meeting thereafter. In other cases, it may take time for key stages of the strategy to progress; updating the board every quarter, or every six months, may be more appropriate.

Consider the measures that should be used—and provided to the board—as a means of tracking progress in strategic execution. Some companies use milestone-based measures of achieving a goal or completing a specific task by a certain date, particularly if they don't expect to see financial results from their strategy initiatives in the short term. Others are able to use financial results as a measure or may incorporate other quantifiable performance measures such as increased market share. Once they are established, determine whether you will include updates on these measures as a regular item in the board's pre-reading materials, even if only for information purposes. Consider, also, whether some of these measures should be incorporated into your annual performance evaluation as CEO.

IN SUMMARY

Many boards regard the oversight of company strategy as their most critical governance responsibility. The approach that the CEO adopts in working with the board on strategy is often a defining moment in the board and CEO relationship—and typically one of the first critical tasks for any new CEO in working with the board. CEOs who present their strategy to the board as a "fait accompli" and fail to engage directors in a meaningful way run significant risks, including a lack of genuine board buy-in and alignment on strategic direction and goals. Steps that can avoid these problems include:

- **Clarifying the rules of engagement on strategy.** Many CEOs tend to limit their directors' engagement in strategic issues for fear of losing control of the process, leaving management as the implementer, rather than the owner, of strategic decisions. Addressing this issue with the board at the outset of strategy discussions can go a long way to resolving this concern. This involves outlining the respective roles in the strategy process and getting the board's confirmation that the choice of corporate strategy lies with the CEO, but underscoring your desire to use directors as thought-partners on strategic issues, thereby leveraging their experience and insight to help you and your team.

- **Engaging the board earlier in the strategy process.** Get input from your directors to find out how they perceive the company's strengths, weaknesses, opportunities, and threats before you start developing strategic alternatives or preparing recommendations. If there are significant differences of opinion between directors and company executives on the very underpinnings of the strategic analysis, it's better to bring these differences to the surface and address them at the outset.

- **Educating the board about key business issues.** Directors cannot engage effectively in strategic discussions if they lack information relative to the company's competitive landscape, industry trends, technological change, the regulatory/political environment, and other issues that provide fundamental context to strategy development. Finding where knowledge gaps may exist can help to determine how best to fill them. Consider innovative ways to provide directors with hands-on experience that can heighten their understanding of your business and of those key business issues that will become the focus of strategic discussions and decision making.

CHAPTER 3

BOARD COMMITTEES— AND HOW TO WORK WITH THEM

NEARLY ALL BOARDS OF PUBLICLY TRADED COMPANIES have three core committees that typically form the backbone of the board's committee structure: Audit, Compensation, and Nominating/Governance. Some boards have more than these three committees, such as Finance, Risk, or Corporate Social Responsibility. Others have adopted different names for the three core committees that may denote an expanded committee role or may reflect the company's heritage. For example, a "Board Affairs Committee" typically includes the functions of a Nominating/Governance Committee; a "Remuneration Committee" is the common British term for the Compensation Committee.

U.S. companies' almost universal adoption of the three core committees stems from the governance rules of the New York Stock Exchange and the Nasdaq, which outline the requirements for committees to oversee each of these three board functions. The stock exchange rules specify, among other things, that each of these three committees be composed *entirely* of outside, independent directors. As such, no CEO or any other member of management who is also a member of the board can serve on any of these three committees.

Nonetheless, it is essential for any CEO to develop a constructive working relationship with each of the board committees and their chairpersons. It is equally important to attend committee meetings from time to time as CEO, even though you are not a committee member—something that can become challenging when the committee meetings take place simultaneously on the afternoon or morning prior to the board meeting, as is often the case.

This chapter will discuss some of the key issues for you to consider in working effectively with your board's committees. It incorporates the views and advice of collaborators with specialized and practical expertise in Audit Committees and Compensation Committees, where noted.

AUDIT COMMITTEE

The Audit Committee section was coauthored by Beverly Behan and Frank J. Borelli. Mr. Borelli has served as Chairman of the Audit Committees of Express Scripts and Genworth Financial, and as the Lead Director of the Interpublic Group of Companies. Earlier in his career he served as the Chief Financial Officer of Marsh & McLennan Companies and was formerly an audit partner at Deloitte Haskins & Sells.

Directors generally view the Audit Committee as the most important and demanding of the three key board committees, given its responsibility to ensure that the company's financial statements are accurate and reliable and that appropriate financial controls are in place. Because the Audit Committee tends to dive into a host of regulatory and financial details in its meetings, many CEOs avoid having much hands-on involvement with this committee—unless they personally came from a finance background—often preferring to delegate the Audit Committee interface to the Chief Financial Officer.

The Audit Committee regularly works with the CFO, controller, head of internal audit, and external auditors. Sarbanes-Oxley requires the Audit Committee to meet alone with the external auditors at least once a quarter: It has increasingly become a best practice for the committee to meet alone with the head of internal audit, the CFO, and the controller once a quarter, as well. It would certainly be a mistake for any CEO to try to insert himself between the committee and the company's financial executives. But it is equally a mistake for any CEO to delegate all dealings with the Audit Committee to his financial team unless, or until, some serious financial-reporting problem looms on the horizon.

Since the fall of Enron, Audit Committees have been deluged with a daunting array of regulatory requirements, and most have put in extraordinary efforts and many extra hours to ensure compliance.

Because of the importance of the Audit Committee's role in governance, the sometimes technical and complex nature of the committee's work in financial oversight (and the fact that other directors rely on this committee to enable them to sleep at night), board members typically hold its chair in very high regard. For this reason alone, it is critical for any CEO to establish a positive and constructive working relationship with the Audit Committee chair.

AUDIT COMMITTEE CHAIR

The director who serves as chair of the Audit Committee will likely have been recruited to the board specifically for this purpose. The Sarbanes-Oxley Act requires all Audit Committees to have at least one member who qualifies as a financial expert, and the commentary to the New York Stock Exchange governance rules require that all Audit Committee members be financially literate and that at least one have accounting or related financial management expertise. Although it is not mandatory to have the financial expert serve as the committee chair, this has become standard practice. In fact, most boards specifically seek a director with a background as a CFO or audit firm partner as their Audit Committee chair, even though the Sarbanes-Oxley definition qualifies a sitting or former CEO and others as financial experts.

Directors with a CFO or professional accounting background who are recruited to a board as Audit Committee chair often serve in this role throughout their entire tenure on the board. If they are invited to join another board, they frequently will be asked to serve on that company's Audit Committee as well. For this reason—and in recognition of the heavy workload involved—some boards, such as that of Campbell's Soup, have adopted governance policies limiting the total number of audit committees on which their members can serve. This issue has also been the subject of commentary in the NYSE governance rules.

There can, however, be advantages in your Audit Committee members serving on other companies' committees as well. Doing so gives them exposure to another board's practices, finance staff, and auditors, which can sometimes provide useful insights and experience, as in situations where your board begins dealing with an auditing or regulatory issue that the other company wrestled with earlier.

If you adopt the practice of one-on-one meetings with all directors, as outlined in chapter 1, meeting with the chair of the Audit Committee at the start of your tenure as CEO will be one of the most important conversations you will have. Even if you are not new to the CEO role, the following can be some useful questions to incorporate into your next, or ongoing, conversations:

- How satisfied is the Audit Committee chair with the performance of the CFO, the controller, and the head of internal audit?
- In what ways have these executives been particularly effective in working with the Audit Committee?
- Does the Audit Committee chair have any concerns about any of the individuals playing these roles?
- Are there areas in which any of these executives could improve their performance?
- What comments does the Audit Committee chair have on the performance of the CFOs of the company's various operating units?
- Does the chair feel the committee gets enough exposure to the operating units' financial executives so as to be comfortable with the company's bench strength in finance?
- Is there anything that the company could do to provide the Audit Committee with better support in fulfilling its mandate?

The answers will provide insights about your finance team and may even reveal ways in which you can potentially improve the Audit Committee's functioning—provided that the cost of additional support the committee might ask for is not prohibitive.

You will also want to explore the chair's views about the external auditors by asking some of these questions:

- How satisfied is the Audit Committee chair with the external auditors and, specifically, with the lead audit partner on the account?
- What is the chair's view on auditor rotation?
- How would the chair describe the working relationship between the external auditors and the company's finance executives?
- Have the external auditors raised any significant issues relative to financial reporting or financial controls with which the chair is uncomfortable?

- Are there any lingering trouble spots or areas of dispute between the external auditors and the company's financial executives?

From discussions with your own finance team, you may already know the answers to some of these questions, but it's useful to get the chair's perspective.

Other questions that you will find useful to discuss relate to the composition of the Audit Committee:

- How satisfied is the Audit Committee chair with the committee members?
- Does the chair feel that more financial acumen is needed?
- By contrast, does the chair recommend opening up Audit Committee membership to some of the board members who lack financial backgrounds but may benefit from serving on the committee?
- Do the committee members put in an appropriate level of effort to prepare for meetings, or do they let the chair do all of the heavy lifting?

EARNINGS PRESS RELEASES

Press releases and other external company communications relating to earnings releases constitute another topic that you will likely want to discuss with the Audit Committee chair—either if you are coming in as a new CEO or if you have a new committee chair coming onto the board or into this role.

Most Audit Committee charters include a provision for the committee to discuss with management the company's press releases that relate to earnings announcements, financial information, and guidance provided to analysts and rating agencies. Start by checking the provision in your own Audit Committee charter to see what it says. These charter provisions stem from New York Stock Exchange requirements, and as such, it's important for the CEO and Audit Committee Chair to get into sync on this issue. This is something that can be worth addressing at the outset of your working relationship: What is the chair's view on the tone of the company's earnings releases? Does she feel that the writing style is too bullish, too conservative, and so forth? Is she satisfied with the way in which the company discloses nonrecurring or important "out of period" increases and decreases to earnings?

New CEOs are sometimes surprised to learn through asking these questions that their predecessors may have fought with the Audit Committee on this issue. If that's the case, you need to bring any lingering tensions to the surface and address them. Asking a new committee chair to review the style of press releases—to ensure right from the outset she is comfortable with them—may prevent issues arising the first time an earnings release is prepared under her watch.

MERGERS AND ACQUISITIONS DUE DILIGENCE

Many CEOs fail to recognize the need to engage and update the Audit Committee around significant activity in Mergers and Acquisitions (M&A). Once the board gives you the green light to pursue an acquisition or merger, the Audit Committee should be briefed on the scope of the due diligence that the company and its advisors are undertaking. Obviously, this is unnecessary for smaller transactions that fall under the level required for board approval. However, where acquisitions are of sufficient magnitude that they have made it onto the board's agenda, due diligence will be an issue very much on the minds of the Audit Committee and its chair.

Don't be surprised—or worse, offended—if the chair asks detailed questions about the due-diligence process you have under way. Better yet, take a proactive approach and have your finance team put together a short document for the Audit Committee, one that outlines the scope of the due diligence in reasonable detail and indicates who will be responsible for each aspect of it—internal company staff, outside lawyers, accountants, and so forth—along with a timeline for the process.

Not only do you want to ensure that the Audit Committee is comfortable with the scope of your due diligence, but this exercise can also be helpful to you, as CEO. This is especially true if the committee identifies a worthwhile area of due diligence not on the list. Even if this doesn't happen, the committee's review and satisfaction with the scope of the due diligence can help increase your own comfort level as well. Too many acquisitions turn out to be unsuccessful because the acquirers were not fully aware of actual and potential weaknesses in the acquisition's business.

RISK OVERSIGHT

Since the onset of the financial crisis in 2008, risk has become one of the hottest topics in corporate governance. The National Association of Corporate Directors published a Blue Ribbon Commission report on risk governance in October 2009, and director conferences, education programs, and dozens of board magazines and journals have featured lectures and articles on the topic of risk oversight. Many discuss the Audit Committee's role in risk oversight.

Nearly all Audit Committee charters contain language giving the committee responsibility for the oversight of major financial risk exposures. This typically stems from a provision in the NYSE corporate governance rules that require Audit Committee charters to include the responsibility to "discuss policies with respect to risk assessment and risk management." However, in the commentary to this rule, the NYSE specifies that the committee should not be the sole body responsible for risk management, but should discuss guidelines and policies by which risk assessment and risk management is undertaken.

In fact, many boards have struggled in recent years with the question of where on the board should responsibility rest for risk oversight. Most audit committees tend to view their responsibility for risk as focused on issues of financial risk and risks to the company and its reputation associated with breakdowns in financial controls—not those risks associated with environmental catastrophes, product tampering, information theft, or the breakdown of critical computer systems.

After the fall of Lehman Brothers, a number of governance pundits advocated the establishment of Risk Committees, a move thus far adopted by less than a tenth of U.S. boards. The more common view on risk is that it deserves the attention and engagement of the entire board. Many CEOs work with their operating people to categorize the company's key risks, rank them from high to low in terms of their impact and likelihood, and then present to the board a half-day session covering each risk in terms of what it is, how likely it is, the potential damage, and what steps the company is taking to address or mitigate it. An alternative approach is to put one major risk item on each board agenda for discussion, so that the full board will have discussed all of them over the course of a year. Still other boards handle this subject by incorporating a risk review into their annual strategy review process.

Regardless of the approach taken, it is useful to understand how your board has been tackling the subject of risk oversight up to now and what role the Audit Committee has been playing in this area. In so doing, ignore the wording of the committee charter and focus on the practical realities of what sorts of risks the committee is actually reviewing and how the members are going about it. And how is the rest of the board reviewing other risk issues? If your company has a chief risk officer, it can be useful to engage this executive in a dialogue about the practices of the Audit Committee and of the board, as a whole, relating to risk issues.

Consider whether the board's current approach to risk issues makes sense. If the Audit Committee is focused entirely on financial risks, how is the company addressing nonfinancial risks? Is this the way that you want to work with your board in fulfilling their risk oversight responsibilities going forward, or are there other alternatives that you'd like to recommend, such as a half-day risk review, a one-risk-issue-per-board-meeting approach, or the formation of a board Risk Committee? Or does it seem preferable to park the subject of risk at the Audit Committee's door and ensure that the members adopt some practices to broaden their risk review beyond financial issues? Can outside resources be helpful to the Audit Committee or the board as a whole in addressing risk issues?

AUDIT COMMITTEE MEETINGS

Try to attend as many of the Audit Committee meetings as you can. Sitting in the committee from time to time puts your finger directly on the pulse of discussions about an issue fundamental to the company's reputation and stock price: the integrity of its financial reporting. However, you should never attempt to hinder, direct, or dominate the meetings. Be prepared to leave partway through so that the committee can meet alone and/or with the CFO, controller, and internal and external auditors. It's a gracious and self-confident gesture when a CEO offers to leave any board committee meeting so as to give the members an opportunity to meet alone.

One of the things to watch in Audit Committee meetings is the performance of its chair and members: Are they asking the right kinds of questions? Do they appear informed and prepared, comfortable engaging in discussions of the complex area of financial controls and reporting? Or are they overly reliant on the external auditors? Do they regularly stray off on tangents rather than focusing on critical issues?

In addition to your own observations, it can be helpful to ask your CFO and head of internal audit for his perspectives on the Audit Committee's performance. Your committee is vitally important to your company and its reputation, and if you lack the talent at that committee table to really do the job, it is something you need to consider addressing with the Nominating/Governance Committee or the Lead Director. For example, Audit Committee members may fit Sarbanes-Oxley's definition of a financial expert, but if none has served in a senior finance or audit role involving a public company it can sometimes create shortcomings in the committee's performance. Alternatively, you may have a committee chair with tremendous expertise in finance management but poor meeting-management skills.

It can be useful to ensure that you and the CFO have some informal communication both in advance of and following the one-on-one meeting that the CFO will have with the Audit Committee at least once a quarter. Those meetings are supposed to focus on financial reporting and controls, but they inevitably get into broader issues—how a particular executive is doing in a new assignment, how the merger integration with "Company X" is proceeding, or whether the investment in Latin America really seems to be paying off. For this reason, it can be useful to touch base with your CFO before she meets with the Audit Committee and to share your perceptions of what broader issues may be on directors' minds. You can also let the CFO know what you've been saying to board members about these issues. In this way, the CFO won't be surprised if some of these topics emerge in her meeting with the Audit Committee and will feel better prepared to respond to them.

It is also worthwhile for the CEO to meet with the head of internal audit on a regular basis. This sets the right tone at the top of the organization, signaling that internal audit issues are important enough to command the ongoing personal interest of the CEO. In these meetings, you will want to ask the internal auditor whether he believes there are any serious deficiencies that operating units are overlooking. It can also be worthwhile to explore his perceptions relative to the operating units' practices in terms of finance—are they conservative to a fault or consistently pushing the envelope?

After the CFO meets with the Audit Committee, touch base to find out what issues were discussed, any concerns the committee raised in the meeting, and what is being done to address them. It is not necessary to have similar discussions with the controller and head of internal audit about their Audit Committee meetings—this may look like overkill and give employees the impression that the CEO is concerned about some kind of financial-reporting problem. However, it can be helpful to ask the CFO to touch base with these executives also, as a means of closing the loop.

If any significant issues have arisen—a finding or deficiency that emerges in a report from internal or external audit—the sooner that the CEO becomes aware of the concern and takes proactive steps to address it, the better. For example, if there is an issue about revenue recognition under particular types of customer contracts, you will want to get on the phone with business units that have these types of contracts and get whatever information you can so that you are in a position to discuss the issue thoroughly with the CFO and external auditors prior to subsequent communications with the Audit Committee.

COMPENSATION COMMITTEE

The Compensation Committee section was coauthored by Beverly Behan and Jeffrey W. Joyce. Mr. Joyce has been an executive-compensation consultant for more than seventeen years and is currently working in the New York office of Frederic W. Cook & Co.

Of the three major board committees, Compensation is the one that nearly always commands the greatest degree of CEO interest—for obvious reasons. It is this committee that determines the pay levels and practices for not only the CEO but also for other members of the executive team, approves the total pool of equity awards for all employees—and often decides board compensation as well. In some cases the Compensation Committee also leads the CEO evaluation and succession planning processes on behalf of the board; in others, those responsibilities lie elsewhere, often with the Nominating/ Governance Committee. It's worth reviewing the terms of the committee charters at the outset to confirm which board committee takes the lead in these areas.

Executive compensation has been a target of shareholder and media backlash for well over a decade. Because of this, it is the area of board responsibility where directors feel most exposure to possible embarrassment. Moreover, those who serve on the Compensation Committee feel a strong sense of responsibility toward their fellow directors, who could be similarly impacted by any negative fallout from decisions that their committee may make. So, while the Audit Committee may seem like the most technical of the board committees, Compensation may seem like the most emotional. Recognizing the heightened sensitivity that board members have around executive compensation is crucial for any CEO, and is a key underpinning of her relationship with the Compensation Committee.

It is also important to remember that, at the end of the day, if your pay practices are egregious, it will most likely be your name and picture in the headlines—and it will be your reputation that is damaged every bit as much, if not more than, the Compensation Committee's or other directors. As such, you have just as much a vested interest in making smart decisions about executive pay as do the Compensation Committee and the Board.

AVOID BEING BLIND-SIDED ON EXECUTIVE COMPENSATION ISSUES

One CEO whom Beverly worked with several years ago was shocked to see his photo in the business section of a prominent newspaper next to a scathing article about executive pay—his pay. He knew that he was well compensated. However, he had no idea that some of the practices his Compensation Committee had adopted in the design of his bonus and stock plans were open to criticism as being "far outside the norm." The CEO felt blind-sided about the entire matter. "Yes, I make a lot of money," he told her, "but I relied on them—the people on my Compensation Committee and the consultants they selected—to get this right. I assumed they had."

Just because the Compensation Committee has ultimate authority for the approval of the executive pay programs does not mean that, as CEO, you should resign from participating in the development of the programs. You have a responsibility to make sure the company's executive pay programs will accomplish their intended objectives while staying within the bounds of good corporate governance practices. Taking the time to increase your working knowledge of executive compensation practices by spending a half a day or so being educated by a compensation expert can be a very worthwhile exercise. This is particularly valuable for a new CEO who, essentially, has inherited the compensation programs endorsed by her predecessor. Not only can this be helpful for engaging with your Compensation Committee on the issues they are wrestling with, but it can inform you of any potential areas of concern within the company's current pay programs.

There is always a question as to whether a CEO should sit down with the board's compensation consultants to undertake this type of session or work with another firm that has no preexisting relationship with the company. There are pros and cons with either approach. The incumbents will have recommended existing pay levels and practices to the Compensation Committee; having done so, they have a vested interest in these practices and may be unlikely to highlight problems with them. However, if you choose to work with a compensation expert who has no preexisting relationship with the company, it is equally important to avoid a bias in the other direction. There may be instances where the new consultant views the engagement as an opportunity to displace the incumbent advisor—offering to do the educational session at no charge and raising every possible problem with the current pay plans in an effort to land the account. Therefore, if you decide that a "fresh pair of eyes" would be helpful in this exercise, you need to discuss the terms of the engagement very clearly up front. Be clear that there is no intention whatsoever to change consultants and pay for all prework and time for the session at the usual rate the consultant would charge any client to avoid the perception that this is a business development opportunity.

If you decide to work with a compensation expert who is not currently involved in providing advice to your board, you will essentially be asking them to take a look at the Compensation Discussion and Analysis (CD&A) disclosure from the proxy and any compensation plan documents that you may have which impact your pay and that of your executive team. From this fairly cursory review, some of the things you might want them to comment on include:

- Is there anything about the company's executive compensation policies or plans that strike them as unusual? If so, in what ways? Do these abnormalities tend to skew executive pay levels upwards or downwards? What is the more typical practice?
- How do the company's executive compensation policies and programs stand up against industry norms, best practices and institutional-investor/proxy advisor preferences? Are there any aspects of

the programs that may be viewed as problematic if the company were targeted by shareholder activists?

- How do the executive compensation policies and programs stand up against current and emerging regulatory requirements, legislation and stock-exchange listing standards?
- Does the peer group of companies that the Compensation Committee has developed seem reasonable or are there companies in the group that clearly seem out of place? A good example of a peer group problem would be a midcap company with several Fortune 500s in its industry included in its peer group—clearly driving up executive compensation averages and opening up the board (and the CEO) to potential criticism. You are not looking to have the outside firm simply refine the peer group by recommending one or two companies to add—you are looking for them to serve as a bell weather on the general reasonableness of the peer group currently in use.
- Having generally reviewed directors' compensation at the company, are there any practices in this area that they would highlight as unusual—either particularly progressive or rather odd?

In the event that you choose to work with the incumbent consultants rather than someone entirely new to the company, the areas of focus will largely be the same. Even though the current consultants may have recommended many of the current practices, it is entirely appropriate for you to ask them if they are unusual in any way. Moreover, if they undertook the executive compensation reviews or other studies on which the current programs are based, ask them to review these with you as well. This may require a little more time in your session, but it enables you to understand fully the basis on which decisions were made relative to current practices. You can also determine how dated some of this work might be and whether it would be worthwhile to revisit any aspect of it—something you may wish to discuss later on with your Compensation Committee chair.

TAP INTO YOUR TOP HUMAN RESOURCES EXECUTIVE

Although executive compensation consultants are hired by, and report to, the Compensation Committee, the senior human resources leader within any company typically plays a major role relative to compensation throughout the organization. For this reason, it is equally important to spend time in some dialogue with this executive on compensation issues.

Legacy practices that continue for grandfathered employees, one-off special arrangements, and compensation programs and policies assumed from acquired companies are just a few examples of circumstances that can give rise to programs that may be flying under the radar. Importantly, these programs could pose a material risk of which executives—and directors—may be unaware. Revised proxy disclosure rules issued by the SEC in 2009 require public companies to include a discussion of their compensation policies and practices for employees to the extent that risks arising from them may have a material effect on the company. As the foundation for understanding whether such risks may exist within the company, most companies have undertaken an inventory of all their compensation programs. As such, this work should be complete and your senior Human Resources (HR) executive should readily have this on hand. If it is not, it needs to be done—quickly.

It is worthwhile to use this inventory in discussions with your top HR executive, not only about exceptions, but also about the alignment of the current compensation programs with the company's business strategy. Some of the questions you may wish to explore in this dialogue include:

- Do the programs support the business values of the company (e.g., are they ethically sound or do they motivate behaviors that may be questionable)?
- Are the programs aligned with the company's strategic goals (e.g., do incentive plan performance measures support financial or other key company objectives)?
- Are the programs aligned with the corporate structure (e.g., domestic vs. global)?
- Are the programs flexible to accommodate change in the operating environment or business strategy?

COMPENSATION PHILOSOPHY

Interestingly, many companies may have no formal compensation philosophy or compensation strategy statement. While proxy disclosure rules require companies to disclose in the CD&A many of the elements that should be present in a compensation strategy, these disclosures are retrospective and explain why something was done in the past. They rarely address the company's pay philosophy going forward.

Once disclosed publicly, CD&A information can take on a life of its own and become the company's de facto compensation philosophy, whether or not a formal pay strategy exists. As such, it is worthwhile to explore whether your company has a formal compensation strategy and whether it is contemporary with the board and management's current perspectives. Some of the key questions that the philosophy should address include:

- What are the objectives of the compensation program as a whole and in terms of each pay element within the program?
- What influence, if any, do accounting, tax, and cash flow considerations have on executive compensation program design?
- What is the company's targeted market positioning of pay?

In terms of the final question, the overwhelming practice is to target total compensation near the middle of the market. However, competitive labor markets, circumstantial factors such as distressed revenue projections, and other factors may lead some companies to target pay at levels above the competitive norm. In these instances, it is critical that a sound business rationale for this be understood and articulated—and that company performance supports the above-market pay posture.

COMPENSATION COMMITTEE CHAIR

In your discussions with the Compensation Committee chair—either as a new CEO or otherwise—some important issues to get her perspective on include the following:

- Are there any current compensation programs or practices that she is uncomfortable with? What are they, and what is the basis of her concern? When was the last time the Committee addressed this issue? What was the outcome? What does she believe needs to occur to address this issue—either a change to the policy or program, itself, or some research to increase her comfort level with it?

- How satisfied is she with the support the Committee receives from its executive compensation consultants? Where has she found the consultants to be particularly helpful? Are there any areas for improvement? Does she support the continuation of the existing consulting relationship?
- How would she describe the working relationship between the executive compensation consultants and the internal human resources executives, particularly the SVP of HR?
- What are her observations and comments relative to the role of the SVP of HR in supporting the work of the Committee? What does she see as the strengths of this executive? What, if any, are areas for improvement? How does she work with the SVP of HR between meetings to review materials and proposals that will be made at the meeting? Does she have any comments relative to improvements in the pre-reading materials for Committee meetings (which are typically assembled by the SVP of HR)?

WORKING WITH YOUR COMPENSATION COMMITTEE

A few practical tips on your ongoing working relationship with the Compensation Committee that may be useful:

- Make sure that the SVP of HR or whoever is supporting the work of the Compensation Committee prepares an annual agenda at the start of each year with specific dates and deliverables. This allows everyone to schedule accordingly; including the outside executive compensation advisors.
- Ensure that the Committee regularly receives information relative to the total compensation of each executive. It can be helpful to present this to the Committee using tally sheets that summarize the level of direct and indirect elements of the annual total pay package, including base salary, bonus, long-term incentives, executive benefits, and potential severance payments.
- Make it a practice to sit alone with the committee at each meeting to exchange candid views about the company's current situation and the impact of these issues in terms of executive pay. These may include financial or other performance issues, executive retention concerns, and so forth.

- It is an equally important practice to regularly step out of the Compensation Committee meetings, enabling the Committee to meet alone or with their outside advisors without management in the room.

IMPLICATIONS OF DODD-FRANK

Executive compensation is a constantly changing part of the governance landscape. One important development that public company boards must now address involves the implications of the Dodd-Frank Wall Street Reform and Consumer Protection Act, which Congress enacted in July 2010, in response to the global financial crisis that began in 2008.

In addition to setting forth sweeping requirements for financial institutions, the Act includes a number of corporate governance and executive compensation reforms that apply to *all* listed U.S. public companies. While some of the provisions of the Act simply legislate standards that were already put in place by the SEC (e.g., director independence, board leadership structure, etc.), others are entirely new and could influence executive pay policies (e.g., disclosure of the ratio of the CEO's annual total pay to the median annual total pay of all employees).

None of the Act's provisions has garnered more attention than the mandated shareholder advisory vote on executive compensation (i.e., the "say-on-pay" vote). For annual meetings occurring on or after January 21, 2011, companies are now required to provide shareholders with a separate nonbinding vote on the approval of the compensation of named executive officers as disclosed in the proxy statement. This vote is required at least every three years. Moreover, at least every six years shareholders must be provided with a separate nonbinding vote on how often the say-on-pay vote should occur (e.g., annually, biennially, or triennially). Shareholders must also be provided a separate nonbinding vote on compensation arrangements for named executive officers related to a change in control, unless these arrangements were subject to a prior say-on-pay vote, when final SEC rules are issued.

While the shareholder vote is nonbinding, it will certainly shape perceptions of the company's executive compensation programs, senior management, and members of the board. As such, it is imperative for any CEO to get out in front of this issue by reviewing the current compensation programs, as we've indicated here, addressing any issues that may be problematic for the company, and ensuring that clear and understandable disclosure of the executive compensation programs is provided in the company's proxy statement.

NOMINATING/GOVERNANCE COMMITTEE

The Nominating/Governance Committee is often considered the "sleeper" of the three board committees by many CEOs, who tend to view the committee's role as largely focused on compliance issues and the creation of relatively formulaic governance policies for posting on the company's website. But in fact, this committee more than any other is the key to achieving tangible and sustainable change in the overall effectiveness of your board. Many of the initiatives that can create meaningful and sustainable change in a board's overall effectiveness lie within the purview of the Nominating/Governance Committee, including director nomination, board evaluation, and individual director evaluation.

BOARD COMPOSITION

If you look at the charters of most Nominating/Governance Committees—including in all likelihood your own—you will see that the Committee's role relative to board composition is often defined as nominating and renominating board members. This rather mechanical description of the Committee's responsibility fails to reflect what (in my view, anyway) is the committee's *true* duty to stockholders, namely to ensure that the Board of Directors comprises the best possible governance team the company can have. Measured against this standard, most Nominating/Governance Committees fall woefully short.

Boards are terrible at performance management. They use retirement ages and term limits to "ease off" underperforming directors—taking out both stars and dogs as they cull the herd—rather than confronting these issues directly. Many have fallen into a paradigm of avoiding any increase in board size. This rationale is used to delay, until a retirement looms, the recruitment of directors who bring much-needed skills to the board table. Consequently, CEOs and shareholders often wait for years before new directors are brought into the boardroom who have backgrounds and experience the company needs for meaningful boardroom dialogue at its stage of growth.

One of the first essential steps you need to take in building your relationship with the Nominating/Governance Committee is to have a candid conversation about the composition of the board. Does the Committee chair feel there is a need for any change to the board's composition? If you were going to add one more director to the board, what skills or experience does the Committee chair feel would be most worthwhile to add? Gauge how closely or far apart you may be on this issue; it may surprise you to learn that you are not actually very far apart at all. If you are, then you need to plant some seeds in terms of the skills and experience that you think would add more value on the board—and explain your reasons for this.

Be careful not to let this conversation degenerate into a dialogue about your wanting to put one of your buddies on the board and/or the Nominating/Governance Chair having designs on recruiting one of his buddies. To avoid this, don't talk about people; talk about skills, experience, or other factors, including, if appropriate, diversity—which can include not only gender and racial diversity but also age diversity and diversity in board composition between active and retired board members. Many boards today are comprised largely of retired executives who have become "professional directors," sitting on two or three boards as their full-time job following an impressive executive career. Don't get me wrong; you need these people. If the company truly faced a crisis, any director with a "day job" would be unable to offer the kind of assistance that a retired board member could step in and provide. However, companies often benefit from having a balance of active and retired executives around their board tables.

Two pieces of homework can be useful prior to this discussion with your Nominating/Governance Committee Chair:

1. Determine whether any of the incumbent directors are approaching retirement age. If one or two will be retiring in the next two or even three years, you might suggest that the Committee consider starting the recruitment process fairly soon rather than on the eve of the impending retirement, a practice many boards tend to follow. While it may temporarily increase the size of the board, planned overlap of the incoming and outgoing board members for a year or two can actually be helpful. In some cases, the outgoing board members can either informally or even formally be asked to mentor the new directors—a practice that is

particularly worthwhile if you decide to recruit an active CEO, CFO, or other active executive with no prior board experience.

2. If the Committee has put together a board composition matrix (or directors skills matrix), take some time to review it. These became popular as a "best practice" more than five years ago and most boards now have them. They are essentially a list of the skills that would be optimal to have around your board table, typically cross-referencing those members of the board who bring each of these capabilities and highlighting any "gaps." Your General Counsel or corporate secretary who supports the work of the Nominating/Governance Committee should be able to give you a copy, if one exists. It will also be important to find out when the skills matrix was created and last reviewed: Is it a fairly recent document, or was it put together five years ago and hasn't been updated since that time?

When you review the skills matrix, consider whether it appears to have been created in an honest effort to put together the best possible portfolio of skills for the Board of Directors to bring to the governance of this company—or does it appear to have been developed simply by cobbling together the backgrounds of the directors now serving on the board. Regardless of the approach taken, consider whether the skills and experience reflected in this matrix truly provide the optimal composition for this board. What's missing? What's on the list that seems unimportant? I once worked with a community bank in Pennsylvania that had "international experience" in their skills matrix. When I asked why, they admitted that they had taken their entire skills matrix from another company on whose board one of their directors also served.

DIRECTOR RECRUITMENT AND ORIENTATION

If some level of director recruitment is in the offing, it's important to talk to the chair of the Nominating/Governance Committee about this process. Ever since 2003, when the New York Stock Exchange and the Nasdaq designated responsibility for director recruitment to an independent committee of board members, the Nominating/Governance Committee has taken a leadership role in this area. That said, it is important for you to discuss what your role, as CEO, should be in the process. The brouhaha between Hewlett Packard and governance watchdog Institutional

Shareholder Services in early 2011 over CEO Leo Apotheker's level of involvement in director recruitment at HP underscores this issue. HP took the unconventional step of creating an ad hoc committee to identify five new director candidates of which Apotheker was a member.

Typically, the CEO is asked to provide input to the Nominating/ Governance Committee about the skills and expertise that she believes would enhance the board's composition and is consulted along the way as lists of candidates are developed. Meeting the CEO is a vital part of the director recruitment process—often a director candidate's most important "litmus test" in terms of accepting or declining a board invitation. Other factors enter the equation as well, such as the stability of the company, its reputation and track record of performance, the caliber of other directors serving on the board—not to mention special circumstances in which a director is appointed by an investor, creditor, or controlling shareholder. Absent such scenarios, however, the candidate's impression of the CEO in terms of the CEO's capabilities and character is often pivotal in a decision to join the board—or not.

This also serves to underscore another change in director recruitment interviews over the past decade. Previously, these were relatively superficial discussions. In fact, once the interview was even arranged, a board invitation was expected. No longer. Director recruitment interviews today are a two-way street—the candidates are interviewing you every bit as much as you are interviewing them. If you do not believe that a director candidate will be effective as a member of your board, be prepared to say so and encourage other directors involved in candidate interviews to do the same. It is a myth that good directors are hard to find. Moreover, it can take years and not an inconsiderable amount of political capital to rid the board of an ineffective director. Be selective.

As CEO, something you should think about, which very few Nominating/Governance Committees consider, is the "recruitment package" that you will send out to prospective board candidates. Once you have identified and approached one or more potential new directors, you will need to send them an information package about the company. This part of the recruitment process is often given scant attention. Typically, the information provided consists of nothing more than the company's latest proxy circular, annual report, and last quarterly financial statement. Yet, in many cases, this is the first package of information they will receive about your company—and they will begin to form impressions from it.

Consider, instead, developing a more comprehensive and well-designed information package for prospective director recruits. Some of the items it could contain in addition to the proxy and annual report might include:

- An overview and history of the company, including major events that have impacted its developments, such as acquisitions, the development of a new product or service offering, expansion nationally and internationally, and so forth.
- Biographical information on all of the board members and members of the company's executive team and a high-level organizational chart.
- Financial analysts' reports on the company over the last twelve to eighteen months. Make sure to include both the positive and negative reports. I always advise prospective directors to research analysts' reports on their own using the Internet or other sources and, once they've reviewed them personally, then ask the company to send over recent analysts' reports. It is a test to see if the company sends both the positive and the negative reports; if only positive reports are included in the package, it is a red flag. This is a company that appears reluctant to share bad news with its board members.
- Major media articles on the company over the past twelve to eighteen months. If there are videos of you being interviewed on Bloomberg, Kramer, CNBC, or other business programs, consider including these as well.

Not only is the prospective candidate likely to be impressed by receiving such a comprehensive information package, this will also serve to underscore that your company is one that takes its board seriously. Anyone who was merely planning to sign up for the director fees and cruise through the meetings on auto pilot need not apply.

Director orientation is another Nominating/Governance Committee responsibility that has a fundamental impact on the overall effectiveness of your board. As discussed in chapter 2, you can hardly expect board members to make a meaningful contribution in strategic discussions and other decision making unless you make a concerted effort to educate them about your business from the time they join your board.

Ten years ago, director orientation was "de minimus." New board members were typically given a binder of materials and asked to show up at the next board meeting. Today, most spend at least one day at company headquarters meeting with the CEO and other key executives. Some boards include meetings or conference calls with each committee chair as part of the orientation program so that the new director has a good understanding of the issues the various committees are dealing with. Others have a practice of asking new board member to attend meetings of all board committees for their first twelve months of board service, only after which are they assigned to a particular committee. This practice may be impractical, however, if committees meet simultaneously prior to the board meeting, as is often the case.

Many boards incorporate a follow-up session into their director orientation program approximately six to nine months later. New board members often feel overwhelmed by all of the information they receive at their orientation and appreciate an opportunity to come back for a second round. At that point, they will have attended a few board meetings and started to get a feel for the company and its business. Questions they will ask in the second round of orientation are often quite different than those in the first. It can be useful to specifically ask the new director what he would find most valuable to cover in one final day of orientation, and then design the second session accordingly.

Incorporating a site visit to a company facility into your director orientation program can be invaluable. However, "rules of the road" should be established at the outset of any director site visits—whether as part of the orientation program or otherwise. When directors make site visits, it is only human nature for employees of all levels within the organization—from senior executives to frontline staff—to express opinions on a variety of issues. Problems can develop if directors are caught off guard and start expressing personal support for the purchase of new equipment or a proposed change to a "stupid company policy." The best response is nearly always for the board member to tell the employee: "I think that's an interesting idea. Have you spoken to the CEO about that? I'll mention it next time I see her." And to do it. After all, it may be something you'd really appreciate knowing about—or it may be something that you are well aware of and are finding tiresome.

Site visits are primarily conducted for the purpose of director education: Board members are not typically sent out as "mystery shoppers" or "employee ombudspeople." Although this may seem self-evident, it should be clarified before the directors board the company jet for the coal mine, the plant, or the call center. Obviously, if board members see facilities in disrepair or hear nothing but a barrage of criticism toward management at every turn, they will form impressions about safety and morale at the company—as they should. However, nothing is more frustrating than a board member who misunderstands the intent of a site visit and returns with a list of some employee's pet grievances that he now feels a personal duty to address.

GOVERNANCE POLICIES

Thus far, we have primarily discussed the "nominating" component of the Nominating/Governance Committee's function—board composition, director recruitment, and orientation. In terms of its governance role, this Committee is responsible for the establishment of governance policies, such as conflicts of interest policies, director retirement ages and term limits, board committee charters, corporate governance guidelines, and the like. The Committee also needs to keep abreast of governance changes in the regulatory environment, including new governance rules of the stock exchanges and the SEC.

This may all sound as dull as dishwater—and in most cases, it is. Therein lies both the problem and the opportunity. Most corporate governance disclosure—be it in the company's proxy circular, annual report, or website—looks and feels like a bunch of boilerplate cobbled together by junior attorneys. There's a reason for that—because in most cases, that's exactly what it is. Hackneyed terms like "stewardship" and "best practices" nearly always turn up in drafting disclosure carefully crafted to say not one word more than is required to achieve compliance with the appropriate regulations.

As you pore over this material, take a different perspective: Look at it as a marketing document to your shareholders about your Board of Directors: What impression does it create? Is the reader likely to feel that this board is a vibrant group who are really on their game? Or do they seem like a sleepy bunch puffing up the fact that they occasionally go "beyond compliance"—as if doing slightly more than the bare regulatory minimum is the best they can offer? Do the biographies of your directors make it evident why each would be well-suited as a member of the board of your company? Or do the descriptions include terms such as "professional director" or "Mr. Wright is the President of F. Wright and Associates"—making you wonder what relevant backgrounds these people actually bring to the board table?

The way you communicate to your shareholders and the public in general about your board and your governance practices should be no different than the way you communicate about your company's products, values, and strategy—doing so to create an impression that you are genuinely committed to excellence, if you really are. There are certainly companies that produce endless rhetoric about their governance commitment in an effort to create this impression. However, as with most false advertising, readers can see through this fairly quickly if there is nothing truly innovative described in their materials. On the other hand, if you have decided to adopt even a handful of the ideas presented in this book, chances are you now have some practices that can set your board apart. Make sure you tell your shareholders about these. For example, if you have created a comprehensive director orientation program, as outlined earlier in this chapter, describe it in your proxy or on your website.

It can also be illuminating to peruse the governance sections of your competitors' websites or proxy circulars—after all, you are typically competing with them for investment capital as well as customer revenues. While you're at it, pull up the websites of some companies renowned for good governance—those who have won governance awards or whose Chairman has just been named "Director of the Year." I am the first to say that just because a board looks good on paper doesn't mean that the board, itself, is effective. Enron, named one of the top five boards in America by a reputable business magazine in 2000, is the classic case in point. However, what these companies are effective at is communicating to outside readers and investors that theirs is a "good board." With that in mind, it's worth taking a look at their approaches.

Don't be surprised if this exercise leaves you brimming with ideas about changes you'd like to make. If it does, your next step is a conversation with your Nominating/Governance Committee chair. If you have a Nonexecutive Chair, make sure that person is also included in this discussion. Provide some examples from the proxies or websites of other companies that impressed you. An initial reaction may simply be to copy the language and approaches these other companies are using. Suggest, instead, that the Nominating/Governance Committee and the corporate secretary undertake a review of this entire issue before changes are made. Two practices that other boards have found helpful:

- **Benchmark Best Practices:** Conduct a benchmarking study of other companies used in your peer group for compensation purposes to examine how they communicate about their governance practices and whether they have policies that are worthy of consideration by your Nominating/Governance Committee. This would be a more structured and comprehensive review than your own perusal of company proxies and websites of about an hour or so—but your preliminary homework will suggest whether a review of this nature might be worthwhile

- **PR Perspective:** Bring the company's public relations, corporate communications, and investor relations professionals into this exercise. This tilts the lens to focus on the actual communication aspect of the governance disclosure—not purely its regulatory compliance function. With the corporate secretary riding herd to ensure that the PR folks don't "push the envelope" to the point that legal or regulatory problems are created, you may be surprised and delighted by some of the innovative ideas that begin to emerge.

BOARD AND DIRECTOR EVALUATIONS

Another area that falls within the ambit of the Nominating/ Governance Committee's governance focus is board and director evaluations. At the annual conference of the National Association of Corporate Directors held in Washington, D.C. in 2009, Phil Laskawy, former CEO of Ernst & Young and Chairman of Fannie Mae, drew applause from the crowd when he stated that board evaluations are a waste of time. In most cases, they are. This is borne out in the findings of the NACD 2009 Public Company Governance Survey of 623 respondents who work with, or serve on, public company boards, two-thirds of whom are outside directors. Only 17 percent considered their board and director evaluation process to be "highly effective" and another 19 percent judged these "not effective."

Board evaluations began as a good idea—an annual process wherein the entire board sat back, considered how effective the board was in governing the company, and decided whether any changes might be warranted. In practice, however, they have degenerated into a yearly "box-ticking" exercise where directors routinely circle a score of three or higher out of five, in response to closed-ended assertions such as: "Our board committees are fulfilling the responsibilities outlined in their charters," or "Our board fulfills its fiduciary duties to shareholders." There are a few write-ins, just for flavor, which enable directors to add a sentence or two, such as, "Pre-reading materials have improved," or "Meetings are dragging on too long."

Typically, results are tabulated into average scores for each item, and the corporate secretary or some other unfortunate person is tasked with the job of analyzing the year-by-year results, desperately looking for some change in the scores to highlight at the board meeting: "Aha! The average on board information last year was only 3.8. This year, it's 4.5. Things have definitely improved."

There is seldom much done with the results. Simply undertaking the exercise serves to fulfill a requirement, under New York Stock Exchange rules, for an annual board evaluation. Most boards are pleased when there appear to be "no real issues" and spend little time discussing the board evaluation once the tabulation is complete. In the next chapter—"Transforming Your Board"—we will discuss a far more comprehensive approach that will highlight significant issues impacting the board's operation, and yield genuine improvement in any board's performance. This approach differs so dramatically from the traditional "box ticking" surveys that most boards don't even consider it to be a board evaluation at all.

As for individual director evaluations—an evaluation of the performance of individual board members—these are less prevalent. Boards that conduct them use a variety of approaches, many of which have significant shortcomings. Popular some years back was an exercise that involved directors evaluating themselves against a list of statements such as, "I ask constructive questions in board meetings," or "I am always mindful of my fiduciary duties in board decision making." Inevitably, the least capable directors often gave themselves high scores, fearing that otherwise their renomination might be in jeopardy. However, the design of the exercise provided no opportunity to counterbalance the individual's own ratings—and often led to considerable eye-rolling in Nominating/Governance committee meetings when the results came in. Due to its evident shortcomings, this approach is far less popular than it once was, although some boards still use it.

Other boards have the Lead Director or Nonexecutive Chair call up each board member and ask them to provide comments on their peers. Although preferable, this approach also has its drawbacks. These conversations tend to be relatively unstructured and often focus primarily on whether someone should be renominated to the board. Board dynamics also play a role. No matter how much the directors may respect the individual soliciting their views, they will routinely "hold their fire" on any issues involving another director they perceive as a close friend of the interviewer—and they are very unlikely to offer much in the way of the interviewer's own shortcomings, even if there are many.

As the Nominating/Governance Committee is responsible for board and director evaluations, you will probably have to get this committee, or at least its chair, on-side if you wish to explore some of the more innovative and impactful approaches in this area that will be discussed later on. Whether you choose to move in this direction or not, it can nonetheless be useful to review the results of board evaluations conducted in the past year or two. If you believe the board needs considerable improvement, you may be shocked to see some high scores in recent board assessments. Don't be. Few board evaluations get to the heart of board performance issues in any meaningful way. It can also be worthwhile to learn whether the board has ever undertaken an individual director evaluation. If so, what approach was used, and what was the board's experience with this exercise?

The Nominating/Governance Committee sometimes receives less attention than the other two major board committees—with Audit and Compensation typically shouldering a heavier workload. Nonetheless, if your goal as CEO is to create a truly great board for your company, this is the committee that you will need to partner with in creating the constructive change necessary to achieve that goal.

OTHER BOARD COMMITTEE ISSUES

Many boards have other committees in addition to Audit, Compensation, and Nominating/Governance. As there is no requirement that other board committees are to be comprised entirely of independent directors, it is not uncommon for the CEO or other management to serve on Strategy or Finance committees, for example, along with some board members.

Executive committees—popular a decade ago—have now fallen into disuse among public companies. While many companies still have them, they rarely meet and are designed primarily to serve as a vehicle to enable the board to respond quickly in some type of crisis situation in which a rapid decision is needed and it is impractical to call the entire board together. These situations are few and far between with today's technology. Executive Committees were criticized as creating a "two tiered" board dynamic, with those who served on the committee taking a more active role in governance than those who did not. This is one of the main reasons they are no longer popular. However, Executive Committees are still commonly found in not-for-profit organizations with large boards of fifteen or more.

One final word on the subject concerns the interface between the board's committees and the board, itself. Specifically, how members of the board—including the CEO—are kept abreast of the work of board committees that they do not serve on. This is a challenge for many boards. Some simply provide non-committee members with the minutes of all committees and encourage them to get in touch with the committee chair if they have questions about the work of a committee they don't serve on. As minutes are typically quite vague, this practice sometimes fails to leave non-committee members feeling truly informed about committee work. At the other extreme, some boards practically rehash the entire committee meeting in the full board meeting. Others have adopted a practice of allowing all directors to attend any committee meetings they wish, whether they are committee members or not. This can become challenging, however, both in terms of committee size and whenever committee meetings are scheduled simultaneously.

Having each committee chair provide a brief update on the committee's work for ten to fifteen minutes at every board meeting is probably the most common practice. However, many boards have begun to supplement this with a comprehensive briefing of an hour or more at the full board once a year, led by the committee chair. Advisors to the committee—such as the external auditors for the Audit Committee or executive compensation consultants for the Compensation Committee—are generally invited to attend and make presentations at these board briefings and to assist the committee chair in developing pre-reading materials for them.

IN SUMMARY

Much of the board's work is done in committees, primarily three committees common to the boards of nearly all publicly traded companies: Audit, Compensation, and Nominating/Governance. Some of the issues you will want to address relative to each of your board committees include:

AUDIT COMMITTEE

- Perceptions of the Audit Committee chair relative to external auditors and your corporate finance team—are there any significant areas of disagreement?
- Alignment on the style and content of earnings press releases— are they too bullish or lacking appropriate disclosure about non-recurring increases or decreases to earnings?
- Providing the Committee with updates on M&A due diligence activities—once the board has green-lighted a major deal, the committee should be briefed on the scope of due diligence and who will be responsible for each aspect of it.
- Clarification of the Audit Committee's role and approach to risk oversight—does the Audit Committee's involvement in risk oversight extend to nonfinancial risks?

COMPENSATION COMMITTEE

- Increasing your working knowledge of executive compensation issues to avoid being blind-sided—this may involve a working session with either your own compensation consultants or other compensation experts who have no preexisting relationship with the company.
- Understanding the board's compensation philosophy or strategy— does one really exist and, if so, does it support the company's business values and strategic goals? Are your compensation programs aligned with the company's strategy and structure?
- Implications of regulatory and other changes in this constantly evolving and highly scrutinized area, such as the recent Dodd-Frank Act.

NOMINATING/GOVERNANCE COMMITTEE

- Perceptions of the Committee relative to board composition—is director recruitment needed to optimize the portfolio of skills and experience at your board table? Consider also the materials that will be provided to prospective director candidates and the design of orientation programs to accelerate a new director's knowledge of the company, its people, and its issues.

- Review your company's governance disclosure (website and proxy circular) through a public relations lens—what impression does your governance disclosure create? Does it sound like a team of lawyers wrote it, or does your board come off looking innovative and "on its game"? How do your governance practices compare with those of competitors or with leading-edge boards renowned for excellence?

CHAPTER 4

TRANSFORMING YOUR BOARD

WHEN CEOS THINK ABOUT "TRANSFORMING" THEIR BOARDS, what typically comes to mind is replacing some of their directors with others who will bring more value into board dialogue and decision making. It's small wonder that changes to board composition figure prominently on many CEO's boardroom agendas: Composition is often the single biggest factor impacting a board's effectiveness—and one that is typically poorly managed by the board, itself. Many boards will continue to renominate directors whose most penetrating boardroom question for years has concerned the color of the corporate jet—until they hit the mandatory retirement age. While inappropriate, the alternative is often considered worse: The awkward conversation in which an accomplished businessperson—and undoubtedly very loyal director—is informed that she is not being renominated for another term.

This chapter will discuss ways to force that conversation. It will also discuss ways to avoid it and still achieve significant changes in your board's composition and overall effectiveness. Moreover, it will broaden the discussion on board transformation beyond the single issue of board membership. There are, in fact, eight factors that contribute to the overall functioning of any board—of which composition is only one. You can have the greatest team of board members ever assembled in terms of their experience and accomplishments, but if you don't give them the right information, if your meetings drone on or focus on the wrong issues, and if the board is not properly engaged in critical areas, such as strategy and succession, you will still end up with an underperforming board and a CEO awash in frustration. Indeed, nothing is more common than a group of boardroom all-stars who fail to function effectively as a governance team.

CREATING CHANGE IN THE BOARDROOM

It takes approximately two years to achieve dramatic and sustainable improvement in board performance. This is never accomplished with lists of best practices or superficial box-ticking surveys where board members rate the board's functioning on a scale of one to five. The implementation of any new boardroom best practice can create an uptick in the functioning of the board. However, a series of piecemeal innovations seldom achieves the impact on overall board effectiveness that is possible with a more comprehensive approach. At some point, if you're really serious about your board, it will be time to get into some depth about how *your* particular board is functioning, where its strengths are, where its shortcomings are, and how you are going to address these in a way that has substantial impact.

Many governance reforms and best practices advocated over the past decade have focused on structural changes to the board: the proportion of independent directors, the requirement for three independent board committees, the creation of an independent board leadership role (Lead Director or Nonexecutive Chair). The reason for this is obvious: These are things that outsiders who have no access to board meetings—regulators, shareholders, governance rating services, the media—can readily see from the company's governance disclosure and use to make judgments about the quality of governance at the company.

There is no question that structural change has an impact on how any board functions—a board of twenty, comprised largely of current or former company executives, is going to function entirely differently than a board of eight who are mostly independent. However, structural impact has its limitations. How the board does its work (board processes) is an equally important dimension in overall board effectiveness. So, too, are the dynamics or culture of the board, and of the board/management relationship.

As the graphic in figure 4.1 illustrates, structural changes can have an impact on board processes and dynamics. However, simply making a structural change is no guarantee of a positive outcome. For example, the appointment of a Nonexecutive Chair is a structural change

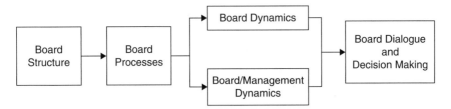

Figure 4.1   Dimensions of Board Transformation

advocated by many as a governance best practice. However, if the board appoints an individual who is ineffective at chairing board meetings (processes) or dominates boardroom conversation to the point that none of the other directors can get a word in edge-wise (dynamics), you can have a very negative result in terms of the board's effectiveness (dialogue and decision making). On the other hand, if the Nonexecutive Chair is an excellent discussion leader (processes) and creates a vibrant boardroom climate (dynamics), this will generally translate into positive results (dialogue and decision making). Moreover, it is possible to achieve changes in the board's overall effectiveness by changing board processes and dynamics without any structural change.

BOARD COMPOSITION: THE MOST IMPACTFUL STRUCTURAL CHANGE

In the past, changing the players at the board table was a simple matter for any CEO. It was the CEO who typically recruited board members and had the difficult conversation when it was time for them to leave. The problem was, many CEOs abused this power—populating their boards with close friends and college cronies and reserving that difficult conversation about leaving the board for those directors who challenged the CEO's proposals and otherwise got in the way. Consequently, the stock exchanges stripped CEOs of this power in 2003, transferring responsibility for director recruitment and renomination to the Nominating/Governance Committee.

Perhaps ironically, CEOs today are not typically looking to repopulate their boards with their sorority sisters; they know those days are gone. Instead, they long to bring directors onto the board who have extensive and current experience in their industry. They pine for a sitting CEO or CFO whose finger is on the pulse of business today. They recognize that a director who has actually worked or done business in a new geographic region, which the company is placing a big bet on entering, could be an invaluable asset. In short, they are looking to bring to the board table experience that could not only add significant value for them, as the company's leaders, but to the company's stockholders.

Many CEOs fixate on the shortcomings of directors they have inherited, hoping to get the agreement of the Nominating/Governance Committee to replace them with board members who have more relevant backgrounds. The problem with this approach is that some CEOs—particularly new CEOs—often spend an extraordinary amount of political capital trying to get rid of some of their directors who haven't said anything at a board meeting in years, or who clearly haven't read or understood the pre-reading materials. While you might expect the Nominating/Governance Committee to champion the cause of changing out an evident underperformer for someone who can make a more substantial contribution, this is seldom the case. Many boards become entrenched: They don't want to have that awkward conversation, instead often responding to the CEO's pleas for change with a reminder that retirements will be upcoming in a few years.

Let's leave aside the rather indelicate question of whether the Nominating/Governance Committee is fulfilling its fiduciary duties to the company's shareholders by taking this position. Let's focus on the easier solution to changing your board's composition—namely, adding the skills and experience you badly need *now* and worrying later on about who's coming off the board.

RECRUIT BEFORE YOU SHOOT

I'm not a fan of big boards. However, neither am I a fan of watching a CEO become embroiled in the detrimental board politics that inevitably accompany an effort to remove directors, particularly when this is often unnecessary to achieve the change you need: bringing aboard some new directors whose backgrounds are likely to make a significant difference to the quality of board dialogue and decision making. Indeed, the addition of only two or three directors can have a major impact.

The starting place for this discussion is your Lead Director or Nominating/Governance Committee chair. Explain that you would find tremendous value in bringing aboard one or two directors who have particular expertise that the board appears to be lacking, and outline how you feel this expertise would make a difference not only for you and your team but to the board, itself. Avoid the trap of naming an individual you have in mind with this very background; the suggestion of any name will smack of the old imperial CEO approach of populating the board with buddies. It is likely to be met with resistance. Keep the issue focused on skills and experience—and try to secure support on this basis.

Once you open up this dialogue, you may find that the Lead Director has her own ideas about other backgrounds that would be helpful to bring to the board table. This can actually lead to a very useful discussion about recruitment priorities. In this conversation, it is important to underscore that you are recommending the *addition* of some new directors; you are not interested in waiting until current board members retire, or in forcing someone to leave in order to make room at the table. Adding one or two board members is seldom problematic unless the board itself is already very large—twelve or more. Even if this is the case, if there are some upcoming retirements, you can point out that it is becoming a best practice to plan some overlap between the outgoing and incoming directors. Besides, it will take time to recruit and orient new directors; if the board size increases during this time frame, the value of bringing much-needed skills into the boardroom and integrating them effectively is probably worth having to endure a temporary bloat in board size.

With just this conversation, many CEOs have managed to put the wheels in motion for new directors with expertise now lacking to be recruited. If you have someone in mind that you believe is a perfect fit for the background you are seeking, you can ask the chair of the Nominating/Governance Committee to consider your recommendation. Some committees will welcome these suggestions; others will be skittish in view of the Hewlett Packard/ISS squabble referenced in chapter 3. The HP scenario illustrates the problems that can develop when any director candidates are viewed as having business ties to the CEO and the CEO is accused of being overly involved in the director recruitment process. What you want to avoid at all costs is any attempt to strong-arm the committee to nominate someone who is perceived to be a friend or pet candidate of the CEO. Any candidate who enters the boardroom this way does so with a cloud over her head that can impact her working relationship with the board for some time. You want your new directors to enter the boardroom with the other members' full endorsement—so that they can immediately have impact.

CAN EXTERNAL DATA BE HELPFUL?

The classic mistake many CEOs make in the area of changing board composition involves waving around a statistic about retirement ages or term limits as the opening volley in this discussion. Directors quickly realize that this argument in favor of governance best practice is just being utilized as a vehicle to repopulate the boardroom. Having seen several CEOs end up in heated exchanges with their Nominating/Governance Committees in taking this approach, my best advice is to open the board composition issue with a discussion about the need for additional experience and skills, which in nearly every case is the real issue anyway.

A couple of exercises to collect additional data can be useful once your discussions with the Nominating/Governance Committee about board composition are under way:

- **Board benchmarking.** This involves analysis of the composition of the boards of other companies in the same peer group that you might use for executive compensation, for example. This is not to say that the backgrounds and experience resident in your competitors' boardrooms ought to govern your choices. However, such studies are always illuminating—often a skill set that never crossed your mind surfaces through this analysis. For example, an international beverage company noted the recent addition of executives from Facebook to the board of Starbucks and from Google to the board of Pepsico, which made them rethink their own director recruitment priorities.

- **Canvass other board members—and executives—about board composition.** This is a straightforward matter of asking this question: "If we were going to bring one new director onto our board, what skills, experience, or background would be most worthwhile to add?" You can focus on this single issue or gather these comments as part of a comprehensive review of the eight components of board effectiveness described later in this chapter. Either way, the responses let you know where the board stands on this issue: Do they share your views about the types of expertise that is needed? Or are there other backgrounds that they consider even more important? It can also be useful to engage members of your executive team who regularly work with the board in this dialogue. Executives typically provide different and interesting perspectives on this topic, often suggesting expertise that may not surface in the board conversations.

READY, AIM...

The concept of "recruit before you shoot" is based on the assumption that the problematic directors on your board are those who simply make a marginal contribution. If you have a board of eight, and three never say much anyway, you essentially have a board of five. However, there are more difficult circumstances in which the problem director is creating a toxic climate in your boardroom.

This can be a boardroom bully, who takes a hostile stance in framing questions, an aggressive or dismissive tone in dealing with management and fellow directors. It may be a director who relishes the role of "constant contrarian"—challenging "on principle" everything that is presented and wasting a lot of precious board time along the way. True contrarians—those who are willing to challenge the prevailing thinking on critical issues—can be some of the most useful directors any CEO can have at the board table. However, those who follow the constant contrarian mantra eat up a lot of board time with unproductive discussion; most have long ago lost their credibility with fellow directors. Or perhaps you have a director who dominates board discussions to the point that hardly anyone else can express a view. All of these are examples of boardroom problems that, because of their negative impact on the dynamics of the board, itself, cannot be ignored.

Dealing with director performance issues is an unsavory job—but it's not your job, as CEO. This responsibility lies with your Lead Director or Nonexecutive Chair. As such, your starting place in addressing the issue is a conversation with her. Let her know that you're concerned about the problem and the impact it's having on the rest of the board. Your goal in this meeting is to convince her to have a quiet word with the director(s) at issue. If you have created a set of board expectations, these can often be a useful reference point for any discussion the Lead Director may have with the director.

It's important to hold a discussion about the performance issue with the Lead Director well before you consider more drastic steps, such as lobbying the Nominating/Governance Committee on renomination. Boards have a tough time telling any director he is not being renominated for another term, and are particularly reluctant to take that step if no one has brought the problematic behavior to the director's attention, giving him a chance to remedy it. However, you may have a situation where the Lead Director is unwilling to confront the matter. Alternatively, she may dutifully take the director aside and mention the concern—but her intervention has no impact, and the problem continues. At that stage, you have two possible options:

- **Lobby on Renomination.** The problem director has been warned—and has chosen not to make any changes. Or he's tried, but the truth is that he is just not making a contribution to the board despite improvement. At this point, you can test the water in some informal conversations with your Lead Director or the chair of the Nominating/Governance Committee on the issue of renomination. It's important to remember that the renomination decision is entirely theirs. However, if the director's behavior is genuinely troubling, if his retirement date is several years away, and if committee members feel that he's been fairly warned about the problem, they may make the tough decision needed.
- **Director Peer Review.** Individual director peer reviews are a valuable tool for the professional development of all board members. If done right, they provide constructive feedback that reinforces strengths and commends significant contributions. They also offer specific and actionable advice for improvement. For this reason, I am always reluctant to see them used as a trap for underperforming directors. When this occurs, the positive aspects of a director peer review can become overshadowed by this potential outcome. That said, they are extremely effective for the purpose of addressing problematic director performance. They are, in fact, one of the only tools that can help address the thorniest director performance issue of all: When the director whose behavior is creating problems is the Lead Director or Nonexecutive Chair.

Director evaluations fall within the purview of the Nominating/ Governance Committee. I have found that in situations where the performance of one or more directors has become the subject of discussion, the Nominating/Governance Committee is often supportive of a process that collects confidential feedback from all board members before making a renominationg decision. Box 4.1, "A Primer on Individual

---

Box 4.1   A Primer on Individual Director Evaluation

If you are considering implementing an individual director evaluation process, there are three important factors to consider in designing it so as to maximize its value to you and your board:

- **Who Sees the Feedback?**

  If one of the reasons you are considering a director evaluation is to address a director performance issue, this will be the most important issue you will grapple with. While it may seem apparent at first blush that you would want the Nominating/Governance Committee to receive a summary of everyone's feedback so that they can use it in their re-nomination decisions, there is an important alternative to consider. That is to position the director evaluation for professional development purposes only, such that directors receive their own feedback—but it is *not* shared with anyone else, including the Lead Director or the Nominating/Governance Committee.

  Most board members respect the comments of their fellow directors and take them to heart, even if they realize that no one else will see their results. The first time I worked with a board who took this approach, one of their directors resigned when he received feedback that he seemed "disengaged" and "unprepared." Although no one else saw these comments, they prompted him to call the Lead Director, admit that he was having significant issues at his own company, and offer to step aside so that the board could replace him with someone who could make a greater commitment. As this example illustrates, this approach enables the director to volunteer his resignation rather than being asked for it.

- **What Format Will be Used?**

  A director self-assessment, where board members rate themselves against a list of criteria such as "I come to meetings well-prepared," or "I ask good questions," has little value in a circumstance in which you plan to use this process to address a performance problem. By contrast, formats that are aimed squarely at the renomination question often achieve little in terms of director development. An example of this is a practice in which the Lead Director calls up each director prior to the proxy being finalized and asks, "Is there anyone we shouldn't renominate?" There is no discussion of any director's strengths and little dialogue about areas for improvement.

  If you are undertaking a director evaluation process, it should not focus entirely on the problematic director; it should provide meaningful feedback to every member of your board. A director peer review, where all board members become engaged in providing comments about the performance of their fellow directors, is the best format to achieve this.

  There are many factors to consider in the design of a director peer review. Although I have used surveys in the past, I abandoned this practice years ago for several reasons: Providing directors with a score on their performance is meaningless. One director who went through this type of evaluation came to the next board meeting demanding to know what his peers meant by rating him a 3.6 out of 5. This format also invites some fairly hostile write-in comments such as, "She is a piece of work," or "Our worst director." These comments create bad feelings and achieve nothing in terms of professional development. An interview format enables these types of remarks to be followed up with such questions as: "Can you give me some examples of what she does or doesn't do that has prompted you to say this person is the worst director you have?" When board members are provided with specific examples, they can understand and potentially address any problems.

- **Who Will Collect and Deliver the Feedback?**

  If you have decided that director feedback will be confidential and *not* be shared with the Nominating/Governance Committee or Lead Director, having a third party both collect and deliver the feedback is the only option to preserve this confidentiality. This can also be a worthwhile approach even if you have decided to provide a summary of the evaluation results to the Nominating/Governance Committee. Where any member of the board becomes involved in gathering the views of directors about their peers, board dynamics that can inhibit candour come into play. Typically, directors hold their fire about the shortcomings of directors considered close friends of the interviewer—or about the interviewer, herself—and are often reluctant to raise sensitive issues, preferring to keep the discussion light and superficial.

  If a third party collects director feedback to maintain objectivity, this doesn't mean that the evaluation results have to be delivered by that party. They certainly can be. Alternatively, if the Nonexecutive Chair, Lead Director, or chair of the Governance Committee is skilled and comfortable in delivering performance reviews, this person can be fully briefed to meet one-on-one with each director to discuss his evaluation once the interviews have been completed and analyzed. Some boards—particularly where there are significant performance issues—ask the third party to meet with all directors first to deliver their feedback, following which the Lead Director meets with one or more board members for further discussion.

Director Evaluation," outlines issues you will need to consider and discuss with the Committee if you decide to go this route.

Individual director evaluations can be a useful tool for any CEO and Nominating/Governance Committee to keep their board at the top of its game. Whenever you undertake this process, your goal should be to provide constructive feedback to all of your directors as an outcome of this exercise. This helps the best directors understand why they are viewed as particularly valuable—and let's face it, everyone likes a well-deserved pat on the back, and most board members seldom get one. It also brings up performance concerns in a way that provides specific examples of the problem so that it can be clearly understood and addressed.

BOARD INFORMATION: A
"QUICK-FIX" PROCESS CHANGE

Addressing board processes often involves some heavy lifting; but these changes typically yield dramatic results. Two areas that most frequently need to be addressed involve the way in which the board engages in strategy and succession planning. In recent years, risk oversight has become a hot topic in many boardrooms. CEO evaluations, quarterly audits, compensation reviews, and board evaluations are all examples of board processes—some of which work effectively, while others require significant change.

One "quick fix" in the area of board processes that is relatively easy to implement and can have significant impact involves changes to your board pre-reading materials. This may seem like an uninspiring topic, but any CEO will immediately get kudos from the board by stepping up to this issue. Many boards are frustrated with their board books but say little to the CEO about this problem. They gripe about it to each other in the limo on the way to the airport or over cocktails at the board dinner, but most feel it's not an important enough issue to bring to the CEO's attention. However, if you actually raise the subject with them, you'll get an earful.

Here's the problem: Most board materials are dense, and the "aha" moment occurs around page 47. Often they are peppered with industry terminology or acronyms that directors aren't familiar with—but feel silly asking about. While financial data is often comprehensive—in some cases over the top—many board books are sparse when it comes to competitor information, industry trends, and similar information relative to the business context in which the company operates.

When working with an energy company in Colorado some years back, I found that every director I interviewed had complaints about their pre-reading materials. These people were really frustrated with their board books and had a lot to say about them. When I finished the interviews and touched base with the CEO, he asked me what I thought the main topics would be for the board offsite. I said, "Well, obviously board information is the biggest issue on everybody's mind and after that—" He stopped me: "Board information?! What's that all about?" When I explained some of the frustrations his directors were having, he was incredulous; none of them had ever mentioned these problems to him.

When we got to the offsite and began this part of the discussion, the CEO led off by stating, "I want to say at the outset that you guys are evidently very frustrated with the board briefing materials, and I get that. But I'm frustrated about this whole situation in another way: I'm frustrated with the fact that everybody was dissatisfied with these board books but nobody ever said anything to me about this."

Take a good, honest look at your last two board books. Try to look at them through the lens of someone who doesn't work day in and day out at the company. Do some immediate areas for improvement spring to mind? It would be surprising if none do.

Raise the issue of pre-reading materials at the end of the board meeting. You can open the discussion by saying, "I've been thinking about making some changes to the board pre-reading packets and I'd like to spend a few minutes getting your thoughts on that. Do you feel that these materials could be improved in any way?"

When directors suggest improvements, ask if they have any samples of other board materials to look at. In the earlier example, two directors got permission to bring in sample materials from other companies whose boards they served on, which the CEO and corporate secretary found very helpful to review. In that instance, much of the directors' concern surrounded the presentation of materials on M&A transactions. They received a lot of financial information about the deals, but very little about the company they were buying—where its major reserves were located in proximity to properties they already owned; biographical information about key executives; the linkage of this particular acquisition with the company's overall growth strategy, and so forth. The samples provided an illustration of how other companies in different industries tackled this issue.

Some of these quick changes to board information can make a big difference:

- Make sure there is a one-page executive summary at the start of every item in the board materials. You may have to ride herd on your executives to get these into place—and make sure they are well done. This means taking the time to read the board books yourself, and pushing back on executives who have not provided a good overview for their materials. While the corporate secretary can also be helpful in the quality control department, nothing makes a more lasting impression, or instills the importance of any new practice, than a call from the CEO.

- Compose a short memo at the start of every board book as your executive summary for the entire meeting. If the meeting has a theme, tell your directors what it is. Focus them on agenda issues that you consider most important and provide highlights of each.

Wherever possible, pose some questions that you'd like directors to consider as they are reviewing the materials. This turns what may previously have been an "information dump" into a guided discussion, typically resulting in far more productive and focused dialogue in the board meeting.

- Police the content of the board books for industry jargon and technical terminology. If these can't be eliminated, create a book of commonly used industry terms for your directors. Many companies have such a book as part of their employee orientation programs—but they never share it with their board. Those who do find that these books become dog-eared in no time.

- Consider the implications of changes to the board pre-reading in terms of presentations in board meetings. If the materials are well organized and comprehensive in the board book, can the presentation in the meeting be pared down? Or can you begin with a few highlight slides and go straight into Q&A?

CHANGING CEO/BOARD DYNAMICS: AUDIENCE OR THOUGHT-PARTNER?

Consider the balance of presentation versus discussion time in your board meetings: Does 80 percent of the meeting consist of presentations with only about 20 percent devoted to dialogue and discussion? If so, small wonder it is difficult to pinpoint meaningful contributions by the board: They spend most of their time listening. Many tactics in terms of agenda design and the reformatting of board information can shift this balance to 50/50. However, the most fundamental shift required to effect this change is the mind-set of the CEO: Do you want to use your board as a thought-partner—in a way that genuinely leverages the talent and experience at your board table—or are you content with them as an audience? If the latter, you will never derive significant value from them.

Some CEOs will argue that until they get the right skill sets around the table, they are wasting their time trying to engage the board as a thought-partner. They feel that their current roster of directors lacks the experience necessary to make a meaningful contribution. There can be some validity to that argument. However, as discussed earlier, there are ways to bring on some new directors who can fill in important knowledge gaps. There are also many ways to derive significantly more value from the board members you already have. Doing both begins with a genuine interest in using your board differently. Even if you undertake the sometimes difficult task of getting the Nominating/Governance Committee on-side to recruit the board talent you need, your gains will be marginal at best if you continue to use the board primarily as an audience for management reports. Once you make the shift, in your own mind, to using the board as a thought-partner, however, everything begins to change in terms of how you work with them.

For example, this shift in dynamics impacts the way in which you bring issues to the board: Rather than presenting an agenda item in finalized form—essentially for approval—you begin to engage the board in discussions on this issue at a slightly earlier point. This is not to abdicate decision making to the board; you should always enter the room with your own well-considered point of view. However, the shift involves your openness to engage in a meaningful dialogue with them—where they might change your mind, or raise issues you hadn't thought of. These are the types of board discussions that CEOs walk away from, thinking, "There was real value in that conversation for me." When you get to that point, you begin to realize what having a great board is all about—and why it was worth the effort.

THE COMPREHENSIVE APPROACH TO BOARD TRANSFORMATION: EIGHT COMPONENTS TO CONSIDER

Up to this point, we have discussed three important areas in which transformation can be achieved—changes in board composition (structure), changes in board information (processes), and a shift in the CEO/board relationship (dynamics). However, the most impactful means of transforming any board involves a comprehensive review of *all* eight factors that contribute to any board's functioning; the engagement of board members and senior executives who regularly interface with the board in this process; and the development of an action plan to address key issues arising from this analysis. This process (see figure 4.2) provides you with a comprehensive overview of the board's current functioning, giving you the lay of the land in the boardroom before you initiate any changes. In many cases, changes that you deem

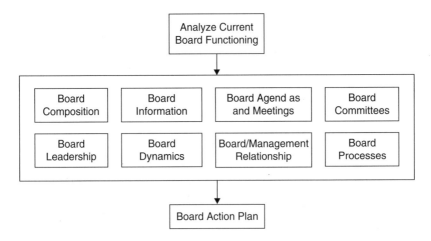

Figure 4.2   Eight Components That Impact Board Effectiveness

necessary after conducting this analysis may differ from the "one-off" changes you might have implemented otherwise.

The types of issues you will want to consider—and get input on from your directors and executives—for each of these eight components include:

- **Board Composition:** Do the skills, experience, and backgrounds of the people gathered at your board table make sense within the context of your company's business model and strategy? Are there evident skills/backgrounds that would make a real difference to include in your board debates—but you haven't been able to add them because you're waiting for upcoming retirements? Or, is yours a situation in which the company has morphed from a regional mono-line to a global conglomerate, yet relatively little change has been made at the company's board table? Do you have directors who "look good on paper," but fail to make a meaningful contribution in the boardroom? How do you go about recruiting board members? What kind of orientation do new directors receive to get them quickly up the learning curve of the company's business? Does the board composition reflect diversity of perspectives—a balance of active versus retired executives, perhaps international perspectives, if this is a key element in corporate growth, and so forth?

- **Board Information:** Most boards today are overloaded with data, primarily myriad financial data, that are often poorly organized and fail to highlight the key points that directors need to focus their attention on. Some CEOs have deliberately adopted this practice as a means of keeping the board in the dark by overwhelming them. Ultimately, however, this is a futile strategy. The quality of board discussion and decision making is directly proportional to the quality of information the board receives. Even if the information is all there—somewhere—failing to organize it succinctly undercuts the value of assembling it in the first place. Board packages have often followed the same format for years. While electronic distribution of information to board members through secure website platforms has become popularized in recent years, a change in the delivery vehicle doesn't address fundamental shortcomings of the content of the information, itself.

- **Board Agendas and Meetings:** Nothing is more common than overpacked agendas with little meaningful dialogue on key issues. What is the balance of presentation versus discussion time in your board meetings? A related issue is the balance of board time devoted to regulatory/compliance issues versus that spent on weightier issues such as strategy and succession. Are the critical issues placed near the front of the agenda, or is that prime slot filled up with compliance issues and committee updates? Do agenda items regularly run over their allotted time—and is this a result of poor agenda design (e.g., fifteen minutes for a review of a major initiative by the second largest business unit) or poor meeting management?

- **Board Leadership:** How effective is the Chair in running the board and committee meetings? Does she draw out different perspectives from around the table on key issues? Or does the Chair dominate the conversation and insist on driving her point home to the exclusion of other views that may be suppressed by her style? Does she know when to call the question on an issue and move on? Or is the board routinely going off on tangents? If you are Chair and CEO of your company, then this component focuses on *your* leadership in the boardroom. Whether the independent board leader is a Nonexecutive Chair or Lead Presiding Director, there are also leadership issues to consider outside of board meetings: How effective is this individual in working with you, as CEO, and with the other directors? Does she keep a finger on the pulse of the board through regular contact between meetings? Are director confidences respected? Is she willing to address thorny issues of director performance, or does she turn a blind eye?

- **Board Committees:** The question here is seldom whether the committee is complying with the terms of its charter but, rather, how effectively the committee is actually functioning. Does the committee chair run effective meetings? Does the committee get good support from company executives and external advisors? What is the interface between the committee and the rest of the board? In other words, how are noncommittee members kept abreast of the committee's work and decision making? Boards take very different approaches in this area: Some rehash nearly entire committee meetings at the full board. Others tell noncommittee members to simply read the committee minutes for an update—a strategy that has backfired more than once when directors not serving on the Compensation Committee were aghast at headlines decrying CEO pay practices at the company.

- **Board Dynamics:** Boards are really all about people—and the working dynamics between those people critically impact the board's overall effectiveness in functioning as a governance team. What is the climate of your boardroom? Is it relatively uninspiring or a vibrant, energized place to exchange ideas and make decisions? Are board members candid or cautious in expressing their views? Has the board become polarized, either through a merger or different generations of directors who have created "camps"? Many boards describe their culture as "collegial," but does that denote an atmosphere of healthy mutual respect, or a clubbiness characterized by "group-think"? Can board members handle conflict and strong differences of opinion? Are challenges and different points of view encouraged, or largely suppressed?

- **Board/Management Relationship:** Is the relationship between the board and management characterized by candor and mutual respect, or do board members behave in a high-handed manner with company executives? Does an atmosphere exist wherein management is comfortable sharing the bad news and tough issues? Does management truly use the board as a thought-partner to wrestle with critical issues? Or is everything presented to the board fairly "buttoned up" with the hope that questions will be minimal? Is management open to the board's advice, or do they immediately become defensive? Has the board fallen into habits of micromanagement, delving into picayune levels of detail that not only wastes board time but leaves company executives constantly feeling "second-guessed"? If this is occurring, does it suggest a misunderstanding of role or a lack of board confidence in the capabilities of the executive team?

- **Board Processes:** This refers to the way that the board engages in some of its most critical areas of oversight and decision making, including corporate strategy, risk, succession planning, and CEO evaluation. Many boards that have the other seven elements in good shape fall short in the area of board processes—which is perhaps ironic, because of all eight components, it is in this area that an effective board can often make its most significant contributions to the company it governs and the executives who lead that company.

IS THIS A BOARD EVALUATION?

Some boards undertake this type of evaluation process every three years as an interview-style board evaluation. In other cases, this exercise has been conducted in conjunction with a new CEO taking the helm, an initial public offering, or the spin-off of a major business unit. Virtually any instance in which corporate or board leadership or board composition has undergone a significant change provides an excellent platform for this type of work.

There are several essentials to using this process in a way that is truly transformative for your board:

- **Objectives.** If your goal is genuinely to use this tool to enable your board to function more effectively, this exercise can go a long way toward helping you achieve it. However, if your goal is primarily a compliance exercise with a new best practice, don't waste your board members' or executives' time with this process. You will reveal important issues through the process that you may not really be prepared to address—and lose credibility if you ignore them.
- **Methodology.** Structured interviews that cover all of the eight components consistently, probing for specifics on each, are

unparalleled in terms of methodology. Having tried surveys, follow-up calls, and web-based tools, my experience is that these all have only marginal impact. To provide some idea of the quality of feedback that should be generated from this process, my interview summary reports, which outline key themes from the analysis, typically run in excess of twenty-five pages with executive summaries. No one finds them dull.

- **Action Planning.** What you do with the feedback you collect from the interviews makes all the difference. There is nothing more common than putting people through a wonderful set of interviews that result in no change whatsoever. To avoid this pitfall, you need to schedule a board discussion of the priority issues that surfaced in the interviews. This not a superficial forty-five-minute agenda item; it needs to be a minimum of two hours.

During this discussion, it's important to offer the board alternatives and recommendations in terms of how to address some of the issues that have been raised—what approaches other boards have taken, for example. It can also be very useful to provide relevant data to set context. If the board is considering the creation of a Risk Committee, for example, you might offer them data on the prevalence of Risk Committees within the S&P 1500, a draft Risk Committee Charter for discussion, and corresponding changes that may be required to the Audit Committee Charter.

Your goal at the end of this working session is to create a Board Action Plan, summarizing what changes are to be implemented, who is responsible for each, and what timeline is set for each initiative to be accomplished. Typically, there should be three to five items on this Action Plan, although many are more extensive than this. The Board Action Plan can be used as a road map to keep these initiatives moving ahead over the next twelve to eighteen months.

IN SUMMARY

When most CEOs think about transforming their boards, what typically comes to mind is replacing some of their current directors with those who bring more relevant experience. However, board composition is only one of eight factors that impact a board's overall functioning—if you fail to address all eight, the board's potential will still be suboptimized.

Creating impactful boardroom change involves not only changes to board structure, but also to board processes and dynamics. Three changes that can have immediate impact include:

- **Adding one or two key directors to fill important boardroom gaps.** Rather than spending political capital trying to oust under-performing board members, adopt a "recruit before you shoot" policy and focus on adding one or two directors who bring experience you need.
- **Upgrading board packets.** One of the quickest ways to improve board effectiveness involves an overhaul to the pre-reading materials. These changes will not only impact the quality of board dialogue, but they can dramatically enhance the efficiency of your meetings.
- **Changing the way you view your board—as a thought-partner, instead of an audience.** If board meetings are 80 percent presentations and only 20 percent dialogue, you are using your board as an audience. Once you begin to view them as a thought-partner, this change in dynamics will profoundly impact the way you work with them, creating far more value.

A comprehensive approach to board transformation involves addressing all eight components:

- **Board composition.** Is the portfolio of skills and experience resident at your board table optimal for overseeing your company? Do your directors "look good on paper" but fail to make a meaningful contribution in the boardroom?
- **Board information.** The quality of board discussion and decision making is directly proportionate to the quality of information the board receives—and whether that information is well-organized, understandable, and focused on the key issues.
- **Board agendas and meetings.** Nothing is more common than overpacked agendas with insufficient time for good board discussion, meetings that run over or routinely go off topic or focus on compliance issues instead of on genuine company priorities.
- **Board committees.** How effectively are the committees functioning? Do they get the support they need from external advisors? What is the interface between the committees and the board,

itself, so that noncommittee members are kept abreast of committee decisions?

- **Board leadership.** How effective is the Chairman (which may be you, if Chairman and CEO roles are combined) in running the meetings? Is the Lead Director or Nonexecutive Chair effective in working with you and interfacing with directors between meetings?

- **Board dynamics.** What is the climate of your boardroom? Is it an open, vibrant place to exchange ideas, or stuffy and uninspiring? Are directors cautious or candid in expressing their views? If the board describes itself as "collegial," does this denote mutual respect or group-think?

- **Board/Management relationship.** Does management view the board as a necessary evil or a valued asset? Has the board fallen into the habit of micromanaging and, if so, does this suggest a misunderstanding of role or a lack of confidence in the executive team? Is management open to advice from the board, or do they become defensive?

- **Board processes.** These refer to how the board fulfills its key responsibilities, including engaging on strategy, succession, risk, CEO evaluation, and similar issues. Many boards that have the other seven elements in good shape fall short here, which is perhaps ironic, given that this is the area where an effective board can often make its most significant contributions.

CHAPTER 5

CEO Succession—The Most Important Decision Your Board Will Make

PERHAPS NO ASPECT OF THE CEO AND BOARD RELATIONSHIP has undergone more dramatic change over the past decade than CEO succession planning. In years gone by, CEO succession was driven almost entirely by the CEO, with fairly minimal board involvement. Boards rarely challenged the CEO's selection of a successor, and they typically ratified that choice with minimal debate, taking the view: "The CEO knows the job and knows his people better than the board ever will. Why would we seek to interfere with the CEO's recommendation?"

This statement is still true today: The CEO does know the job and his people better than the board ever will. Yet, as boards have become more engaged over the past decade, they have looked to play a more assertive role in CEO succession planning. After all, the choice of CEO is the single most important decision any board will make (apart from the sale of the company, or a very significant merger or acquisition). In the National Association of Corporate Directors' 2009 Public Company Governance Survey, over 90 percent of respondents rated CEO succession planning as a "critical" or "important" board responsibility. However, when asked to rate their own boards in the area of CEO succession planning, only 16 percent said they were "highly effective," while nearly 30 percent rated themselves as "not effective" in this critical area.

Boards are still largely finding their way in the area of CEO succession planning. They recognize the vital importance of this decision in terms of its impact on the company and its shareholders. They are no longer content to make it without having done their own due diligence to select the best candidate, and they are instituting rigorous succession planning processes. However, most are still experimenting with different approaches. Therein lies both the challenge and the opportunity for today's CEO: to help the board put in place an effective CEO succession planning process that enables directors to arrive at the best succession decision without feeling that they are relinquishing control of the process to the CEO along the way.

Perhaps ironically, in the past three years, more than half of my CEO succession planning assignments have been initiated, not by the board, but by the CEO. In fairness, some of these resulted from situations in which the board told the CEO to get the process started. In other cases, the CEO felt that the board was dragging its heels on succession and feared that when the time came to designate a successor, directors would either force him to defer a planned retirement date or go outside to recruit a replacement simply because they hadn't spent enough time overseeing the development of internal candidates. In more than a few instances, the CEO was genuinely concerned about whom the board would choose to succeed him, stating: "I don't feel the board really knows my people very well at all, and I have a real concern that they are going to choose the person they are most comfortable with—such as the general counsel—rather than the person who is really the best qualified to take over the leadership of this company from me." Once a succession planning process gets under way, these fears are often substantiated.

CEOs Are Often Shocked by Directors' Perceptions of Key Executives

Several years ago, I worked with the board of a founder-led technology company preparing to undertake an initial public offering. The board had governed the company for seven years as a private entity, so directors had the same level of exposure to board issues and members of the executive team as any public company board might have had. Because the founder—a forty-three-year-old entrepreneur—was so critical to the company's success, the board needed to discuss emergency succession planning: What would happen if he were hit by a bus? Yet board members resisted the discussion. "Our CEO is in his early 40s," they told me. "We have far more important issues to talk about right now. Let's not waste time with that."

The board offsite was held in Colorado, and a day of skiing preceded the formal meetings. In the late afternoon, I sat in the hotel bar at the foot of the mountain with two directors. We watched as a snowboarder came flying down the hill at breakneck speed. When he reached the bottom and lifted his goggles, we all recognized him: the CEO. "And you guys don't think you need to talk about emergency CEO succession planning?" I asked.

The following morning, one of the directors mentioned the CEO's impressive snowboarding run and conceded that it might make sense to have a discussion about emergency succession after all. Other board members were still resistant; one of the venture capitalists serving on the board rolled his eyes and said, "Look, we all know who would run this company if something happened to Jim." I suggested that to put the matter behind us and make sure there was complete agreement, I'd simply count to three and everyone would name that person. Then we could move on. On the count of three, the directors volunteered four different names. One of the names electrified the CEO: "*George?* You guys think *George* can run this company? You know, I haven't said anything to the board about this, but I've been thinking of firing George. His numbers have been terrible lately, and what really bothers me is that when you raise issues with him, he makes a lot of excuses. The other people on my team don't respect this guy at all. And now that we're into this—even after we IPO, I will still be a major stockholder. If something really were to happen to me, my family's future depends on this company's success. So I have a pretty big stake in making sure you guys make the right decision about who would run it. I think we do need to talk about this."

While the impact of a bad CEO-succession decision can be especially profound in the case of a founder-led company, any CEO becomes concerned when learning that the board's succession thinking is off base. Recently, the board of a mid cap healthcare company undertook an emergency succession planning exercise when the CEO became president of the national industry association, raising his profile and making him a likely target for recruitment by Fortune 500 competitors with deep pockets. As the CEO and board were entirely open about the possibility of this situation, they decided it would be worthwhile to engage all directors and executives in a series of interviews to get every-one's candid feedback about what should happen if the board were faced with this situation.

The CEO and executive team were in complete alignment as to who should be appointed as interim CEO if the current CEO were recruited away. Among other things, they noted that in these circumstances a company needs a chief who is a particularly effective communicator with internal and external audiences, has solid industry experience, and is credible with Wall Street and government regulators. Al, the company's CFO, had the whole package. Moreover, there were other strong executives on the team who could support Al in different ways in leading the company if this situation arose, bringing stability to a difficult situation and furthering the implementation of the current strategy.

But the directors disagreed. They viewed Al as a poor communica-tor and questioned how he managed to hold his own with Wall Street analysts. While board members viewed other executive team members as capable in their current roles, few were considered to have CEO potential; those who did were many years away from having the experi-ence and credibility needed to take the corporate helm. If the current CEO were to depart, board members planned to appoint one of the outside directors who had neither chief executive nor industry experi-ence as interim CEO to "hold down the fort" while they launched an external search for a permanent replacement.

The current CEO was shocked to learn about the direction board members were heading. He was also deeply concerned about the direc-tors' opinions of his executives, which had surfaced in these discussions, particularly their perceptions of Al, the CFO. But after spending a few days considering his board's assessments, he developed some insights as to what was underlying their perceptions: The CFO behaved differ-ently in board meetings than he did in meetings of the executive team or meetings with financial analysts. "You know, Al and I have sort of a partnership in how we lead this company," he told me. "When we are with the executive team, we operate almost like coleaders. When it comes to Wall Street, obviously I take the lead on certain things as CEO, but I view that largely as his show. And he views the board as my show. Of course, he presents the financial results and other financings we need their approval on, but he really plays a more passive role in the boardroom than he does elsewhere. But the board never sees him out-side of the boardroom, other than perhaps at a company social event or board dinner. So of course they are drawing conclusions about him from what they see in board meetings, which don't reflect his capabilities at all."

The exercise prompted a critical discussion between the CEO and his directors. He told them that he understood why they had drawn these conclusions about Al, but urged them to remain open-minded about the CFO's capabilities. He suggested that board members listen in on some upcoming analysts' calls to hear Al talking to Wall Street. He also spoke with Al, told him how directors were reacting to him, and suggested that he change his approach in board meetings. After only six months, the board had changed their views about Al—and their thoughts on the emergency CEO succession plan.

This example underscores the fact that board members tend to see company executives through a very narrow window. One of the most important things today's CEOs need to do in working with their boards on succession is to open that window wide enough to ensure that the board is making the right choice based on leadership capabilities that the company needs—not based on boardroom style or comfort level. In succession contests, boards often favor executives with whom they have the greatest amount of interaction—and hence the greatest comfort level. The CFO and general counsel attend board meetings more regularly than those who run operating divisions, which can bias directors to favor them. One CEO was stunned to learn that the directors considered his general counsel a top contender to succeed him. "He's a great general counsel and a great guy. But he's never run a P&L and manages a staff of about fifteen people. Who are they kidding?" That is not to say that executives who occupy top staff roles are poor choices to become CEO, particularly if given assignments to broaden their experience on the operating side. But this comfort factor should underscore that "opening the window" may also require the CEO to give executives who are infrequent board meeting attendees greater exposure so as to create a more level playing field among succession candidates.

TWO KINDS OF CEO SUCCESSION PLANS

There are two different types of CEO succession plans that boards need to consider and put into place with input from the CEO:

   a. **Emergency Plan:** An emergency succession plan, the infamous hit-by-a-bus crisis plan, enables the board to respond quickly and effectively in naming a successor. As discussed in chapter 1, a new CEO should address emergency succession planning within her first nine months in the job. But even if this has not occurred, emergency CEO succession planning can come onto the board agenda at any point in the CEO's tenure—and should be reviewed at least annually after a plan has been developed.

b. **Retirement Plan:** The retirement succession plan, a far more comprehensive process, extends over a period of three to five years. The retirement succession plan involves the development of criteria for the next CEO, assessment of internal (and, as appropriate, external) candidates against those criteria, development of candidates as appropriate, a successor selection, and a plan for the CEO transition itself.

EMERGENCY CEO SUCCESSION PLANNING

I have never actually heard of a CEO being hit by a bus. But there are dozens of examples of companies that found themselves suddenly without their chief executive for a variety of very different reasons: corporate scandals/SEC investigations (Enron, Tyco, AIG), sudden death or illness (McDonald's, Lazard Frères, Sara Lee), firing (General Motors), resignation (Bank of America), criminal indictment (Martha Stewart Omnicom), sex scandal (Hewlett-Packard, Boeing), a hotel fire that killed most of the executive team (Arrow Electronics)—and the list goes on.

While it may initially seem counterintuitive for a CEO to urge the board to plan for a scenario that involves him being out of the picture, there are several important reasons for any CEO to champion the board's development of an emergency succession plan:

- Conducting an emergency CEO succession planning exercise with the board can provide the CEO with valuable insights as to how directors view members of the executive team. Examples outlined earlier illustrate how this knowledge enabled the CEOs in those instances to address some important misperceptions on the part of the board about their executives. In other instances, this intelligence has served to arm a CEO with the knowledge he needed to fire a top executive when he realized that his assumptions about the executive's relationship with the board were

inaccurate. Regardless of what surfaces, this exercise seldom fails
to yield some eye-opening comments.

- Most CEOs are highly committed to the organizations they
lead. If something really did happen to them unexpectedly,
they'd want the company to which they've devoted their energy
and effort left in the best possible hands. As highlighted in the
example of the snowboarding CEO about to take his company
public, this can become an even more important factor if the
wealth of the CEO's family will remain linked to the company's
fortunes.

- Boards will often delay succession planning when things are
going well, hoping to put off the inevitable conversation about
retirement because they fear being unable to find someone as
capable as the current CEO to replace him. While some CEOs
relish the thought of extending their tenure, others want to retire
at a certain point and make a gracious exit. Emergency succession
planning is an excellent vehicle to kick-start the long-term succession discussion with the board.

Some emergency succession discussions are quite perfunctory. The
CEO comes to the board and says, "If something were to happen to
me, I recommend Bill or Sue to step in as CEO on an interim basis."
The board and CEO discuss the relative merits of the candidate(s)
suggested and come to agreement, allowing flexibility depending on
the circumstances of any emergency that may actually arise. Even a
simple conversation of this nature will leave the CEO and board with
the semblance of a working plan that they can reference in the event of
an emergency. It's better than nothing.

However, you will get a lot more juice from an emergency succession planning exercise if you design it to include some or all of these
elements:

a. **Develop some criteria for the choice of interim CEO:** This
need not be a complex process with matrices and competency
models. Simply identifying three or four important criteria
for someone who could credibly step in to lead the company
in a crisis is all that is needed. Taking this step forces the
board and the CEO to stand back for a moment and develop
some objective requirements for leadership before diving

into the merits of various individuals. It also provides a useful yardstick and context for a discussion of the individuals against the criteria, which can sometimes lead to a different decision—and potentially form the basis of some long-term CEO succession planning work.

b. **Gather feedback on potential candidates from each director in advance of the board discussion:** As noted above, from the standpoint of the CEO, the most valuable aspect of the emergency succession planning process is typically the insight it yields about how the board views the members of her team. Individual director interviews prior to the meeting nearly always offer greater candor and more specific comments about company executives than can ever be achieved during a group discussion in a board meeting. It also shows the CEO the lay of the land about where directors stand on various executives in advance of the board conversation.

c. **Determine whether any candidate is ready to be named CEO as a permanent replacement:** If you are in the last stages of a CEO succession process—perhaps twelve to eighteen months away from a planned retirement—the board may be entirely comfortable naming the top candidate as a permanent replacement should an emergency arise. If not, the directors will probably want to name someone as interim CEO while they consider their options for a permanent replacement. In these circumstances, the interim CEO may be a member of the executive team, a board member, a former company CEO brought back from retirement, or someone else entirely. Simply discussing whether the appointment would be permanent or interim may change the decision about who should be named. Some boards are entirely comfortable appointing their most promising executive to the interim CEO role; others fear that by doing so, they may embarrass and lose this key executive if she is not ultimately ratified as the permanent CEO. If there is no permanent CEO candidate within the executive ranks, a "silent search" (described later in this chapter) may also be a tactic to consider.

d. **Broaden the discussion to two or three other mission-critical executives:** Consider expanding the emergency succession discussion beyond the CEO to two or three other key players whose sudden loss would create significant concern—potentially the

CFO, Chief Operating Officer (COO), chief merchant (in retail organizations), chief technologist/scientist (in high-tech or biotech), and so forth. Among other things, such conversations can have implications for the board's exposure to the "understudy" executives for these critical roles. For example, the CEO of a regional bank whose board I worked with on this issue recommended Mark Wiggins, the controller, as the emergency replacement for the CFO. Directors frowned. "Who is Mark Wiggins?" they asked, noting that they'd never met him. Wiggins was invited to make a presentation at the next board meeting.

e. **Consider the scandal/plane crash scenario:** This involves planning for the most unthinkable of all—a situation involving the loss or "neutralization" of the entire executive team. Whether it is a tragedy, such as a hotel fire or allegations of corporate wrongdoing, that creates this crisis scenario, this is a situation where someone from the board must immediately step into a leadership role because no one on the executive team can. If a Lead Director has been appointed, or if the roles of chairman and CEO are split, there is often an assumption that the Lead Director or Nonexecutive Chair will step in should a crisis of this nature ensue. But not always—and this is worth discussing. For example, the board of a mid cap chemical company had an outstanding Presiding Director who was a scientist and professor. When the board entered into this conversation, the Presiding Director indicated that he would not be comfortable serving as interim CEO because he'd never run a public company. He felt that two other board members who had been CEOs earlier in their careers would be better choices should the situation arise. Time commitment and geographic location can also be important considerations: If your Lead Director is based in California and your company is in Maine, you may prefer to consider someone resident in the Northeast who can quickly come to corporate headquarters and stay there for whatever period is required to stabilize the situation. The scandal/plane crash discussion can also serve to highlight gaps in board composition. For example, after this conversation, a board that lacked directors with significant industry background was finally galvanized to recruit a director from the industry.

KEEP THE PLAN CONFIDENTIAL

Regardless of the components included, the emergency CEO succession plan should never be shared beyond the CEO and board members. Even executives who regularly attend board meetings should be excluded from this discussion, whether or not they are candidates to step in as CEO in a crisis. In exceptional cases, the general counsel or Senior Vice President of HR may be asked to stay in the boardroom for the emergency succession planning conversation. However, if this is your choice, you need to ensure that this executive understands the necessity of confidentiality.

Why is confidentiality important? Because, inevitably, dynamics and expectations change when word leaks out who has been designated an emergency successor to the CEO. The individual chosen may feel he is next in line when the CEO retires. But this is sometimes not the case at all: He may simply have been the best choice at the time the plan was last discussed. As time passes and other executives are recruited or developed with long-term CEO succession in mind, the plan may change—and often does. It's unavoidably awkward to inform a key executive: "We had initially chosen you to step in as CEO in a crisis, but now we feel it should be Judy." Better to keep the plan confidential in the first place.

One CEO decided that he wanted to be entirely transparent with his executive team about this issue. The emergency successor upon whom he and the board agreed was the CFO, and it was determined that this would be an interim appointment. As the CFO and CEO were roughly the same age, it seemed evident that the CFO would not be the CEO's ultimate successor at retirement. He was simply the best choice to take the corporate reins should a crisis arise. As such, the CEO saw no harm in sharing this information with the CFO and his other direct reports. He put the topic of emergency CEO succession on the agenda for his next executive-team meeting and took pride in his openness.

But three years later, the CEO began planning for retirement, and the board decided to change the emergency CEO succession plan: If something happened to the CEO at this stage, the top candidate to become his successor at retirement (the head of a major business unit) would be named interim CEO. This change in the emergency plan created a quandary for the CEO. On the one hand, he felt he should tell the CFO—and his other top executives—about the change. After all, transparency was his hallmark. On the other hand, he and the board did not want to prematurely signal their choice for his permanent successor, and sharing the new emergency plan would bring this to light. He chose to say nothing—and fortunately, nothing happened to him between that time and the day his permanent successor was finally named president and COO.

Some CEOs argue that they need to make sure the individual designated to assume leadership in a crisis is willing to shoulder the mantle. "After all," one CEO told me, "we may all think Michael is the best choice to step in if something happened to me, but I'm not sure he would be willing to do it." Most CEOs know their executives well and have a pretty good sense of whether someone would be willing to take the helm in an emergency. If an actual crisis hits, such as that which befell McDonald's or Lazard, executives typically put their shoulders to the wheel instead of running for the tall grass. More often than not, checking it out with the executive is simply an excuse to share the "good news" with the person named. For all the reasons noted above, it is a temptation best avoided.

If there are legitimate concerns about someone's willingness to assume leadership in a crisis scenario, there are easy ways to address them at the outset of the emergency-succession discussion, rather than after the decision is made. Here are two examples:

- The CEO of a retail company told his executive team, "At the board meeting next week, we are going to talk about who could step in to run this company if I were hit by a bus. Obviously, all of your names and the names of some of the board members will be raised in this discussion. I will not be able to share our decision with you, as we may change that decision over time. What I'd like to know is this: If I were hit by a bus next week and the Presiding Director called you and asked you to step in as CEO of our company, are there any of you who would not be willing or able to take this on? Is there anyone who wants to take their name right off the table for our discussion next week?" As he suspected, one executive raised his hand and said, "My son is about to undergo surgery, as many of you know. Please take my name off the table. I have no illusions, by the way, that I would be the person chosen to step in as CEO if something happened to you. But since you asked, I certainly could not take that on right now."

- In another instance, the board and CEO of a branded-goods company hired me to help them develop their emergency CEO succession plan. This involved interviews with all board members to get their perspectives in advance. Similar interviews were conducted with members of the executive team. In each of the executive interviews, participants discussed their own willingness—and readiness—to step in as CEO in a crisis. This provided important input for the CEO and board on many levels.

IMPROVING BOARD RESPONSE TIME IN A CEO CRISIS

While there are many collateral benefits to emergency CEO succession planning, the primary reason for undertaking this work is to put the board in a position to respond quickly and effectively if an emergency should arise. With that in mind, there are two things a CEO should insist on when working with her board on emergency succession planning:

1. Drive the board to a tentative decision as to whom it would name as interim or permanent successor in the event of a crisis.

Boards will balk at this. After all, the decision point is the place where succession discussions become contentious. "We have many good people on our executive team," they will argue. "We will choose the right person if and when an actual crisis erupts. Why waste a lot of time arguing over that now?"

A board's ability to respond to the sudden loss of a company's CEO within forty-eight hours makes all the difference in terms of instilling confidence in employees, shareholders, customers, and the general public. Boards that have done this when faced with the sudden loss of their CEO have not only distinguished themselves as models of "good governance"—their swift decision making often prevented the myriad problems that can accompany the loss of a CEO, among them employee confusion and a sharp drop in stock prices.

Contrast Bank of America (B of A), which indeed had good people on the executive bench behind CEO Ken Lewis. One of them was Brian Moynihan, whom the board eventually selected as Lewis's permanent successor. However, that decision came months after the CEO's sudden resignation announcement and following scathing criticism for the board's evident lack of preparation when it was unable to respond sooner. Some defended B of A's board by pointing out that many of their directors were relatively new and therefore unable to name a permanent replacement to Lewis quickly. This is true. But it would have made a big difference and have restored a great deal of confidence in the board and the company had they named an interim CEO within forty-eight hours of Lewis's calling it quits. Several company executives and board members had solid credentials to serve in this role.

Getting directors' agreement on who they would actually name in a crisis (either as interim or permanent CEO) puts the board in a far better position to be able to respond within forty-eight hours. It doesn't mean they will actually follow through on this decision should an emergency occur. They may make a different choice entirely, or drag their feet after all. But forcing them to a decision point increases the chances of a quick response, and that is one of the best things you can do to safeguard your company and protect your shareholders if something should happen to you.

2. Develop a logistics plan as a component of the emergency CEO succession plan.

While emergency CEO succession planning discussions typically focus on the issue of who would step in as interim or permanent CEO, it is equally important to map out the steps for the board to communicate with key stakeholders at this critical time. This requires a lot more than a telephone tree of who-calls-whom if tragedy strikes. The logistics plan should include details of who will contact which stakeholders, how and when, over the initial days and weeks following a crisis.

Although the identity of the emergency CEO successor should remain confidential for the reasons outlined earlier, some company executives and advisors should be involved in the development of the logistics portion of the emergency CEO succession plan. The company's legal counsel should be asked to verify requirements for notifying the stock exchange(s), regulators, and any other bodies required by law to receive notice of a material change in the company's situation. Public relations (PR) professionals are also worth consulting on various aspects of the logistics plan. Internal PR and communications staff will be on the front lines in the event of a crisis. As such, it can be useful to engage them in planning for it. External PR advisors can frequently offer perspectives on how other companies have handled various communications issues during an emergency. These can also be factored into the logistics aspect of the plan.

USING A SILENT SEARCH IN
EMERGENCY CEO SUCCESSION PLANNING

Companies with a relatively new CEO, or one who is nowhere near retirement age, often lack executives who, in an emergency, could readily step in as a permanent CEO replacement. This is particularly true among mid cap companies that—unlike General Electric, PepsiCo, and Procter & Gamble with their many large business units—simply do not have the luxury of keeping a team of CEO-ready executives at the top of the house. For these companies, the emergency CEO succession plan may involve naming an interim CEO and embarking on an outside search for a permanent replacement. To accelerate the outside search process, some boards factor a silent search into their emergency CEO succession planning activities.

The concept of a silent search is this: The board and CEO put together a list of external candidates who appear well qualified to serve as CEO of the company. In some situations, a search firm is retained to either create or expand the list. No calls are made to develop the list or determine whether any potential candidate has interest in becoming CEO of the company; it is done entirely from individual awareness of key players in the industry and public or search-firm databases. A silent search serves as nothing more than a vehicle to give the board a starting place if it actually faces the emergency loss of the CEO and believes there is no one in the company immediately ready to serve as a permanent replacement.

One board that found great value in a silent search was NYSE Euronext. Marsh Carter, Chairman of the NYSE prior to the Euronext merger (and Deputy Chairman thereafter), initiated a silent search at a time when the board felt it was vulnerable to losing then-CEO John Thain. Directors retained a boutique search firm to develop a list of potential CEO candidates, with the provision that no calls be made to stir up speculation that the board was considering a CEO replacement. Once the list was developed, Carter and Thain reviewed and discussed it. Afterwards, the list was stored in a vault by the general counsel and updated regularly.

Some time later, the very situation that the NYSE Euronext board had anticipated came to pass: CEO Thain was recruited to take the helm at Merrill Lynch. Dusting off the silent search, the board noted Duncan Niederauer's name close to the top of the list. Niederauer had been working as an executive at NYSE Euronext for about a year at the time the silent search was developed and was considered to be doing well; in fact, appointing him as permanent CEO of the Exchange was now a real possibility. It was the silent search that sealed the board's decision. Once the silent search results were circulated, board members quickly saw that their top internal candidate was entirely competitive with outside talent. In this way, a board of more than twenty directors, spread out over the United States and Europe, was able to name the CEO's replacement within ten minutes after the announcement of his resignation to become Chairman and CEO of Merrill Lynch.

CEO SUCCESSION PLANNING FOR RETIREMENT

While most CEOs wish they never had to vacate the corner office, others practically cross dates off their calendars in anticipation of a time when they can relax and do "some of the things I've always wanted time for"—travel, teaching, writing, spending more time with family. Whether the concept of retirement is a welcome or dreaded one, there is one thing nearly all CEOs have in common when they think about retirement: They want the board's choice of their successor to be the right one—someone who will build on their accomplishments as chief executive and chart a successful path for the company to which they've devoted so much of their time, energy, and talent.

Many CEOs who are finally of an age where retirement is no longer a distant mirage have told me that nothing keeps them up at night more than the idea of their board selecting as their successor some hopelessly inappropriate executive the directors have simply taken a shine to. Or, watching their board recruit an outsider who is a terrible fit for the company and its culture—causing talented executives (that they have nurtured) to leave, making bad strategic choices and essentially destroying the company.

As noted at the start of this chapter, boards and CEOs today work together very differently on CEO succession planning than in the past. Yet, while boards now insist on a greater level of engagement in CEO succession planning, the CEO retains a critical role in the process. Among other things, the CEO needs to make sure that the succession planning process is one about which directors themselves feel comfortable. Only then will they truly be confident in the new CEO they have selected, and will genuinely give that person their support. This is one of the kindest things you can do for your successor—and something you may have appreciated if your predecessor did it for you.

Reflecting on the process that the board used in your own selection as CEO is often a good starting place in thinking about succession planning for your own retirement: What worked well from your perspective as a candidate—apart from the obvious outcome in the board's brilliant decision to name you as CEO? What didn't work well? What steps did they put you through that you'd never want to make your successor endure? What were the other pluses and pitfalls of the succession process you underwent? How many of your current board members were on the board at the time when you were appointed—and therefore are familiar with the process used in the last CEO succession?

Once you have made some preliminary observations about what worked and didn't work the last time, it can be helpful to put these in the context of a CEO succession planning framework. There are five steps in any long-term CEO succession plan.

1. DEVELOPING CRITERIA FOR THE NEXT CEO

This the cornerstone of any CEO succession plan—and one that seldom gets the attention it deserves. Criteria should be tailored to reflect the company's business model, long-term strategy, and desired culture. They should also encompass both work experience needed for someone to be successful in leading the company as well as capabilities or competencies that the individual should possess. The "experience" component often gets down to the need for P&L experience, international/global experience, experience working in one or more of the company's key businesses or industries, brand management, or knowledge of a core science fundamental to the company's business.

In developing this list of CEO capabilities, the term "leadership" always surfaces. But "leadership" means different things to different people and there are underlying components of leadership that need to be clarified to define what appropriate leadership would be for your company going forward: Is this someone who has a directive or collaborative leadership style? Is a good leader for this company someone who develops people well, delegates a lot of responsibility to them, and holds them accountable? Or someone who keeps control of key issues so that there is little doubt who is in charge? Are there different requirements for the next CEO to be effective in leading the company internally and representing the company externally?

The fundamental mistake at this early stage is a failure to engage *all* board members in the development of the CEO criteria. Often, the CEO or the board's HR committee puts together a list of CEO criteria—or asks the senior HR executive to do so. This list is then presented to the board for comments, typically resulting in a cursory review and some minor edits. Therein lies the problem: As the time approaches for an actual CEO succession choice, directors wake up and review those criteria in a new light, often recognizing the absence of some important items and suggesting that some of the criteria on the list aren't really very important at all. When this happens, the entire succession process can be upended, taking on an entirely different— and sometimes shocking—direction.

One way to avoid this problem, and make sure you have the criteria that can form a good cornerstone of your succession plan, is right at the outset to engage all the directors in developing the CEO criteria. Have someone interview every board member at some length three to five years before your anticipated retirement date—discussing not only the requirements for the next CEO, but also the CEO succession planning process itself. You can hire an experienced third party for this purpose or delegate the interviewing task to a seasoned HR executive in-house whom the board trusts and respects and who is not viewed as an internal CEO candidate.

As CEO, not only should you be included in the interview process, but your insights should carry considerable weight in the development of the criteria, because nobody knows the job better than you. Consider extending the interviews on future CEO criteria to key members of your executive team, including those who may become internal candidates as your successor. Cynics sometimes fear that interviewing internal candidates may skew the process, as they may try to focus CEO criteria toward those aligned to their own experience and capabilities. But there are two reasons to include them: One of the biggest fears any CEO confronts in succession planning is losing top executives who aren't chosen to become the company's next leader. Engaging them in the development of CEO criteria can actually help to keep them on board, by giving them a say in the requirements for future leadership. Moreover, top executives nearly always bring valuable and often different perspectives than those of the directors—perspectives that are worthwhile bringing to the surface and considering in criteria development.

Granted, the rapid pace of change in business today causes some CEOs and directors to become skeptical about developing the future CEO criteria too far in advance. "What might be our priorities in selecting a leader today could change entirely a year from now, depending on some of the developments in our industry," the chairman of the HR Committee of a mining-company board recently explained. He's not wrong. But if you take this argument too seriously, you would delay developing CEO criteria until a few months prior to your succession decision. At that stage, you may discover that some of your top internal candidates lack the skills or experience you require—and that you now lack the time to give them assignments to fill in those gaps, forcing you to hire a CEO from outside the company or to extend the current CEO's tenure. In the latter case, you are hardly in a different position than if in the first place you had developed CEO criteria two or three years prior to the initial retirement date.

Developing the future CEO criteria three to five years out at least gives you something to work with in terms of the assessment and development of your succession candidate pool so that you can get those parts of the succession process under way. And you need to start somewhere. Once you've developed the criteria, you and your board should regularly review and refine them. They may need a substantial overhaul if the company's strategy changes significantly; in other cases, they will not change much at all over time.

It is equally essential to engage the board in prioritizing the criteria: Which are the must-haves for the next CEO, as opposed to the nice-to-haves? Nothing is more common than ending up with a list of criteria that are unrealistic if not fantastical: Our next CEO must leap tall buildings, walk on water, wake up nightly with Steve Jobs–worthy product inspirations, and give galvanizing company speeches that rival Barack Obama's. For this reason, once the criteria are developed it's critical to do a reality check with the board: What are the four or five really important requirements for the next leader of this company? In my experience, rather than the criteria significantly changing over time, it is most often the prioritization that changes with changes in the company's business, industry, or the economic environment in which it operates. Something that was a nice-to-have two years earlier is now a must-have, and vice versa.

2. ASSESSING INTERNAL CANDIDATES AGAINST THE CEO CRITERIA

Once the criteria for the future CEO are developed and agreed upon, the next step is to assess possible internal candidates against those criteria, using three lenses:

- **The lens of the CEO.** The CEO knows the job and knows her people well. As such, one of the most critical things for any CEO to offer the board shortly after establishing the criteria for future leadership is an assessment of internal candidates against those criteria.
- **The lens of the board.** The board is ultimately responsible for the CEO succession decision. Directly or indirectly, directors will be assessing internal executives against the criteria established for the CEO job. It is therefore useful to elicit the board's perspective on internal candidates at various stages in the succession process. This also underscores the need—throughout the succession planning process—to provide directors with meaningful exposure to the internal candidates. This will be discussed later in this chapter.
- **The lens of a third-party executive assessment:** Third-party assessments are increasingly viewed as proper due diligence from which a board can benefit prior to making what is arguably its single most important decision. There are a number of

reasons why these assessments can be helpful in CEO succession planning:

- **They almost never fail to provide useful insights about candidates.** Often, they serve to confirm the gut feeling that board members and/or the CEO have about a particular candidate. In other cases, the assessment may serve to highlight an executive's strengths and positive "matches," with the criteria, which may previously have been overlooked.

- **They help to overcome issues of candidates who "show well" in board interactions but lack essential capabilities.** Many boards have made bad CEO succession decisions by selecting a charismatic, polished executive who lacks fundamental capabilities, or one with whom directors are comfortable because they've had a lot of interaction with her over the years. Assessing candidates against established criteria in a third-party assessment can neutralize this problem by focusing objectively on each candidate's fit with the criteria. It can also reveal shortcomings that a candidate's likeability can obscure.

- **They can be particularly useful in executive-development decisions.** By highlighting both the executive's strengths and shortcomings with regard to his preparedness to become CEO—and evaluating these against the criteria for the job—assessment results can help the current CEO and senior HR leader to determine whether, and if, those shortcomings can be addressed through job assignments, coaching/mentoring, and other means. Assessments can also provide insights to the CEO that can be useful in mentoring top succession candidates, an activity that often takes more of the CEO's time and attention as the succession approaches.

However, there can be downsides to using executive assessments, and several important factors need to be considered to implement them successfully. The major downside is that assessments—or the views of any third party about any CEO candidate—should *never* replace the board's judgment about the choice of CEO. This is an easy trap for many boards to fall into, particularly those comfortable with reliance on outside experts. To avoid it, make clear at the outset that the assessment is not the basis for selection of the next CEO but, rather, one of several lenses through which directors should view CEO candidates. Some of the questions that often arise relative to using executive assessments in CEO succession planning are addressed in the sidebar (see box 5.1).

3. PUTTING DEVELOPMENT
PLANS IN PLACE FOR TOP CANDIDATES

Once you've had a chance to review your high-potential internal CEO candidates through these three lenses—the CEO's, the board's, and

---

Box 5.1   Using Executive Assessments in
CEO Succession Planning: Frequently Asked Questions

Will an executive assessment that was conducted as part of the company's leadership-development program suffice for CEO succession planning purposes?

Many companies have their senior managers and executives regularly undergo third-party assessments as part of ongoing leadership-development programs. Reviewing these assessments will undoubtedly provide useful insights about internal CEO candidates. However, what these ongoing assessments lack is a specific evaluation of the candidate against the CEO criteria.

If executive assessments will be a component of CEO succession planning, when should they be conducted?

There are several schools of thought on this issue. The first is to conduct them right after developing the CEO criteria. This will enable the results to be used in creating development plans for the candidates who most closely match the CEO criteria. It may even reveal one or more internal CEO candidates who had not previously been considered, but who fit the CEO criteria very well. If this happens, the new candidates can be included in the pool for the purposes of development and ongoing board exposure—something that would not have occurred had the executive assessments been deferred until the decision point.

Another school of thought is that the executive assessments should be part of a final "package" on each candidate and conducted closer to the time when the board will actually choose the new CEO. A third approach is to conduct executive assessments more than once throughout the succession planning process—once at the outset of the process to assess candidate development and again later to aid the board in its final decision.

What's the best way to find a credible third party to conduct these assessments?

Only someone who has experience conducting executive assessments and presenting them at the board level will have the credibility to be effective in working with the senior team and board for the purposes of CEO succession planning. There are many assessment specialists who lack board experience or say they have "done CEO succession planning" when, in fact, their experience has been limited to succession planning for the CEO of a business unit, which is quite different.

It is, therefore, advisable to ask any firm or individual you are considering for this assignment to provide references at three levels for each company offered as a reference: the CEO (either current or former), the senior HR leader, and a board member. There may be instances in which the senior HR leader was excluded from the succession planning process (for example, if he was a CEO candidate, or if the board had confidentiality concerns about keeping *all* executives out of the succession process). As such, there is nothing to worry about if this explanation is offered for a lack of a senior HR reference at one or more companies. However, an experienced third party should be able to provide all three levels of references for at least one client.

What are the best executive-assessment tools for CEO succession planning?

Once you've found an experienced assessment professional with whom you're comfortable working, the CEO, top HR leader, and whichever board committee is taking the lead on CEO succession planning (be it the HR Committee or Nominating/Governance Committee) should discuss in detail with the third party what suite of tools will be used in the assessment process. Some companies use a single executive-assessment tool, such as a 360 or a behavioral event interview tailored to the CEO criteria. Others use a suite of tools to provide multiple lenses on each candidate. In selecting your tool kit, factors to consider include:

- **Scientific validity.** The executive assessment specialist should be able to point to data that establish the validity of tools that she uses and recommends.
- **Easily understood.** The tools should yield results that both executives and board members can readily grasp and practically utilize. Confusing or vague models, charts, and/or terminology are apt to be misinterpreted or disregarded altogether.
- **Linkage to CEO criteria.** One or more of the tools should be focused specifically on measuring each executive's capabilities against the criteria established for the future CEO.
- **User-friendly for participants.** The process should be interesting, relatively enjoyable, and above all, insightful when participants receive their results. A process that uses *only* web-based assessment tools tends to be too limited for CEO succession planning and is typically poorly accepted by senior officers. There should be some interview or other one-on-one components factored in.

The use of a 360 is often one of the more controversial components in designing executive assessments. Advocates feel that 360s broaden the window on an executive's leadership by gathering feedback from peers and direct reports. Detractors feel that subordinates and peers may be less than forthright in providing 360 feedback, either afraid to say anything negative for fear of retribution, or overly critical due to personal agendas. The use of 360s or 360-like feedback (such as climate surveys) is typically an important discussion in establishing the final suite of tools in an executive assessment.

Once the assessment tools have been chosen, it can be beneficial for the CEO to personally undergo an assessment before any of the candidates do so. This not only enables you to understand the assessment process firsthand and work out any kinks, but the trial assessment can sometimes highlight factors that made you successful in the role of CEO. These may even be capabilities of which you are unconscious but that have significantly contributed to your success. If this happens, it may be useful to reconsider the CEO criteria and modify them to incorporate some key factors that the assessment process may have brought to the surface. Trial assessments have also been helpful to CEOs in giving them information about themselves that can assist them in mentoring CEO candidates.

the third-party's assessments—you need to consider what development opportunities, if any, you will provide them between now and the time when the board will select the next CEO. Your goal at this stage is typically to consider how you might be able to address any gaps between their abilities/experience and the CEO criteria, which is typically done through work assignments, coaching or mentoring. At this point in an executive's career, training programs or courses are generally of limited value; meaningful development initiatives typically consist of:

- **Developmental job assignments.** This frequently involves taking high-potential executives who have spent most of their careers in staff roles, such as finance or legal, and providing them with some level of operational, P&L experience. In other cases, it may involve an international assignment in which living and working in another country has been identified as an important requirement for the next CEO to have. Where a company has multiple business lines, it may involve an assignment to a business unit in which the executive has had no prior experience.

  It takes time to provide meaningful job assignments to any candidate. An international or cross-company posting of six months, for example, is unlikely to accomplish much, whereas an eighteen-month or two-year assignment will have definite impact. This is one of the most important reasons to start the CEO succession planning process early on—at least three to five years prior to the planned retirement date.

- **Mentoring by the CEO.** The CEO's mentoring of internal candidates often provides their most powerful professional-development experiences. In considering how to groom your own successor, reflect back on what your predecessor did for you—or didn't do: What was the most helpful experience or advice she gave you? What would have prepared you better to step into the corner office? One of the challenges many CEOs experience at this phase of the succession process is delegating some of their responsibilities to the candidates they are grooming—such as having them take the lead on an analysts' call or represent the company at a major industry conference. Yet, these can become critical developmental experiences, and your constructive feedback to the candidates on their performance in handling them can be essential to their development.

- **Executive coaching.** Coaching has its fans and its detractors. However, if an internal candidate's shortcomings are largely in the areas of leadership style and interpersonal effectiveness, it may be worth considering. If the candidate already has a coach, it can be very useful for the CEO to meet with him and outline some of the gaps to focus on in working with the candidate going forward. Ask for the coach's ideas on how to address these shortcomings, and whether he feels that it is reasonable to expect the candidate to be able to make these types of changes. If the coach has worked with the candidate for some time, insights from this conversation can be especially enlightening.

BOARD EXPOSURE TO INTERNAL SUCCESSION CANDIDATES

Throughout the succession planning process, it will be important to find ways of giving board members meaningful exposure to internal CEO candidates. Traditional vehicles include having them make presentations at board meetings, participate in board offsites, and attend board dinners. Increasingly popular is the practice of having one or more directors come to the executive's area of responsibility on a site visit unaccompanied by the CEO. This enables board members to interact with the executive on her own turf and observe how the candidate's subordinates react to her. Directors may be invited to watch the candidate deliver a presentation at a shareholder road show or a speech at an industry conference. Some companies will invite a board member to attend a global meeting of a top candidate's division. Often, the director participates in the internal meeting by addressing the employees as part of the proceedings, but the director's real objective is to watch the candidate in action with the divisional team.

Frontier Communications Corporation Chairman and CEO Maggie Wilderotter, currently a director of Xerox and Procter & Gamble, has introduced an innovative board mentoring program at Frontier. Each director is assigned to serve as a mentor to one of the CEO's direct reports or to a high-potential candidate. Directors are asked to meet with their mentees at least three times a year outside of board meetings. Typically, they do this over a meal, to allow them to get to know each other one-on-one in a more informal setting. These meetings enable the board member to gain a deeper understanding of the executive, who in turn is provided with the benefit of the director's experience on whatever issues they discuss. Further, the director acquires in this way a more in-depth understanding of the company's operations. None of these conversations are to involve compensation—or, needless to say, career counseling about moving out of the company—and all are completely confidential. Assignments are switched every two or three years, allowing board members to have a mentor relationship with more than one person (some board members are on their third mentee) and avoiding a director feeling that she is a particular executive's sponsor when it comes to succession decisions. Input from each executive's mentor is solicited when Frontier conducts its annual succession planning review.

Frontier also structures its board meetings throughout the year with a view to giving directors extensive exposure to candidates, not only for CEO succession, but for the other C-suite roles. Two candidates are identified as potential successors for Wilderotter and each of her six direct reports—a total of fourteen executives whom the board gains an opportunity to get to know. Frontier holds at least six board meetings annually, and each meeting typically features four presentations from key executives on different aspects of the company's business. This yields at least twenty-four opportunities for executives to present at board meetings over the course of a year. Meetings are planned so that each of the dozen C-suite succession candidates gets at least one of these opportunities to present to the board. Formal board meetings are often followed by a dinner at which an array of Frontier executives, often from around the country, are introduced to the board. Finally, at least one board meeting is held in a market Frontier serves, allowing the board to meet local company talent along with local officials and customers.

Even traditional board dinners lend themselves to refinements that can make them much more worthwhile. In an interview for my *Bloomberg* BusinessWeek column, INSEAD dean Frank Brown offered some insights on this topic that are worth repeating here. He suggests matching up the executives at board dinners, helmet-to-helmet, with the outside directors: For example, if there are nine outside directors, the CEO should invite nine executives to the dinner. Executives should be a mix of the CEO's direct reports and up-and-coming stars. Board members should be given information in advance about each of the executives who will be attending the board dinner, and the CEO should encourage directors to do a little homework, prior to the dinner, on each executive's area of responsibility. For example, if one of the attendees will be the SVP for Latin America, directors should be encouraged to read up on political and economic developments in that region so that they can discuss some of these issues with the executive over drinks or dinner. It can even be worthwhile for the CEO's office to send some relevant articles to board members in advance of the dinner, including media articles on any of the executive attendees.

Board members are often concerned about the types of questions or issues they can properly raise with executives at these dinners. Given the opportunity to spend time getting to know a potential CEO or C-suite succession candidate over dinner, directors generally want to engage in dialogue about something more meaningful than movies, sports, and restaurants. But they are concerned about asking any CEO's subordinate to express views on the company's strategy or performance—and rightly so. These are inappropriate questions that can put the executive in an awkward position. However, there are many questions that directors can and should consider asking company executives, the answers to which will provide greater insight into how the executives think about business issues. It can be very useful for the CEO to offer a list of these types of questions to board members, which might include some of the following:

- Tell me about growth opportunities that you see in your business.
- What trends do you see as either fostering or inhibiting these opportunities for growth?
- What are the biggest challenges you are facing right now in your business?
- What do you see as the major risks facing your area of operations, and how are these being addressed?

It will be important to give the board exposure to not only those candidates who may become your successor as CEO, but also to those who may be on deck for other key C-suite positions so that the board takes comfort in having bench strength at the top of the house. In any CEO succession planning process, one of the board's concerns—and yours—will be the flight-risk of those executives not chosen as the next CEO. Directors will want some insights into the pipeline of talent available to replace the candidate who may ultimately be selected for the corner office as well as those who may pack their bags to become CEO somewhere else.

The traditional means of briefing a board on bench strength involves the senior HR executive compiling a binder that includes photos and CVs of two possible successors for each C-suite position. The binders look impressive, but often fail to provide board members with much insight about the readiness of these candidates to take on the new role. The best way to avoid this criticism is to take the same approach on bench strength that you take in succession planning for the CEO position itself. Develop criteria for each of the senior executive roles and provide an assessment of the candidates against these criteria. Where there are gaps, indicate what development initiatives are under way. These may involve development of top internal candidates and/or hiring from the outside to create a more viable candidate pool.

4. DECIDING WHETHER TO ENGAGE IN AN EXTERNAL SEARCH FOR OUTSIDE CEO CANDIDATES

One of the most profound changes in the area of CEO succession planning over the past decade has been the dramatic shift to a preference for, and selection of, internal candidates to become CEO, rather than hiring a CEO from outside the company. A 2008 Booz and Co. study of CEO appointments in the top 2,500 global companies found that 65 percent were internal promotions, 20 percent came from the outside, and 15 percent were what Booz referred to as "apprentices"—internal promotions of executives who had been hired into the company within three years prior to their appointment as CEO.

The apprenticeship model is worth consideration. If you begin your CEO succession planning efforts three to five years in advance and find considerable gaps between your internal candidates' capabilities and the CEO criteria, you have time to hire one or more candidates into the company in a senior executive role and include them in a development process along with the other internal candidates. This can serve to smooth the transition; give you, the board, and your executive team meaningful exposure to this person in executive roles over two or more years; and ensure that there is a good cultural fit between the individual and the organization—always a concern when an outsider is brought in directly as the new corporate leader. However, this is not an option if you don't begin succession planning until one or two years before a CEO succession decision: Anyone hired in at that stage is hired either as CEO or for a short transitional period of six to twelve months.

Among your board members, you may find two very different schools of thought on the subject of external search—and whether one should be included in the CEO succession plan, particularly where there are high-potential internal candidates: Some board members feel that an external search is required due diligence on the board's most important decision—namely, the choice of CEO—and want to include one in the succession planning process regardless of the caliber of internal executives. Others, though, feel that when the company has identified and developed some strong internal candidates, external searches are not worth the money typically required to include them. They also worry about internal candidates' reaction to news that the board is looking outside.

Even CEOs to whom the thought of going outside for their replacement is anathema should not ignore this question. It will be on the minds of your board members, and if you don't raise it, one of them eventually will. In considering it, the first question is the timing of an external search: Will an external search be conducted three to five years out in order to identify and recruit some additional talent into the company's internal pool as part of an apprenticeship model? Or will the decision about conducting an external search be deferred until a date closer to the actual choice of successor—a sort of final due diligence in the succession planning process? Deferring the question can enable the board to gauge the progress of internal candidates before committing to an external search. In these circumstances, it is not uncommon for advocates of looking outside to change their views if they have become satisfied with the capabilities of internal candidates. By the same token, if internal candidates have faltered, those of the let's-not-spend-the-money camp may be the first to offer headhunter references.

Remember, also, that a benchmarking study—such as the silent search used by NYSE Euronext for emergency CEO succession planning purposes—might be worth considering, either as a first step or even an alternative to a full-fledged external CEO search process.

If the board decides to incorporate an external search into the succession planning process, managing this issue with internal candidates typically falls to the CEO. In working with the board on this issue, there are two critical items to consider:

- **Avoid secrecy.** Some board members may recommend that the external search be conducted without informing any of the internal candidates. Indeed, I am aware of one board that made this approach work. They were ultimately unhappy with all of the external candidates, and the internal candidates never learned about the search until after it was over.

  However, I recommend being entirely open with the internal candidates about an external search. These are big boys and girls—they know that this is the board's most important decision and can hardly be surprised to hear: "The board feels it has an obligation to shareholders to conduct an external search as part of our CEO succession planning process. It is by no means a reflection of any unhappiness with our internal talent or a feeling that going outside is preferable to promoting from within. They just see this as part of their due diligence. I wanted you to be aware of this." Far better to be up-front than run the risk of having the search discovered through company gossip or similar channels, yielding all kinds of damaging speculation and a general feeling that the board is not being forthright with the company executives—hardly a promising start to the CEO/board relationship of an internal candidate who may ultimately be chosen.

- **Strive for a level playing field.** While this will never be entirely possible to create, there are several important considerations in trying to make the comparison between internal and external candidates by the board of directors as fair as possible.

  The first is simply to ensure that the CEO criteria used to identify, assess, and develop internal candidates is the same as that used to identify and assess external candidates. If the CEO and board used the type of comprehensive process described earlier in this chapter to derive and prioritize the CEO criteria—and conscientiously reviewed and updated these annually, or whenever warranted by a shift in strategy or other material change in company circumstances—there should be no reason to use something different.

The second involves creating an assessment process for external candidates that parallels that used with internal candidates. This gets back to the suite of assessment tools discussed earlier. Some of these tools, such as 360s, cannot be used for external candidates for obvious reasons, but others can and should be. This is a discussion that you should have with the board at the outset of any external search. If your senior HR person has been involved throughout the succession planning process, it may be valuable to get his input on this issue, as well.

Finally, consider whether internal candidates will be offered a board interview for the CEO job similar to interviews that will be offered to external candidates. There can be a tendency for directors to be dismissive of this idea, on the basis that they know the internal candidates well enough already. Indeed, if you have been giving board members the types exposure to internal candidates outlined earlier in this chapter, that argument may be sound. But there is merit in holding interviews with internal candidates all the same: It will be seen as unfair, by not only the candidate but the entire executive team, if an outside candidate is chosen as CEO without this courtesy being extended to internal candidates.

5. CHOOSING THE NEXT CEO AND PLANNING THE LEADERSHIP TRANSITION

Unless an outside candidate is hired directly into a company as its CEO, the first step in a succession decision is typically the top candidate's elevation to the role of President and COO. This signals not only to the rest of the company but to investors and other stakeholders that this is the front-runner to become the next CEO. The appointment as President and COO is an opportunity to give this individual operation-wide responsibility, typically for a defined period of time prior to the board's final succession decision.

The appropriate period of time for a CEO successor to serve as President and COO is a subject of considerable debate. In most cases, the job lasts only about a year and is used largely as a CEO-in-waiting type of role. In other cases, the COO is a "real job" and final proving ground that can last three years or even more.

Covance Chairman and CEO Joe Herring spent three years as the company's Chief Operating Officer before being named chief executive. He became convinced that this is a far preferable practice than the one-year, heir-apparent approach, because his lengthier tenure as COO enabled him to take on meaningful projects of companywide responsibility that better prepared him to become CEO. "If you're in that job for three or four years, the candidate has to step up, make it a real job, and demonstrate some tangible accomplishments in that job," Herring explains. "That's a really good test for any candidate—and it also helps the candidate. When I became CEO after serving as COO for three years, I felt really ready for the CEO job. In fact, if my predecessor hadn't stayed on as Chairman for a transitional period after that, I would have been just fine because I'd developed a real comfort level working with the board, with Wall Street, and with the executive team in the time I was COO."

Your preference on the length and usage of the Chief Operating Officer role can make a big difference on the timing on your succession plan itself. If you are planning to appoint your successor to the COO position for twelve months before the final transition, then a three-to-five-year time horizon to start the plan should work well. If you prefer the idea of using the COO position as a "real job," and having the candidate serve in that role for three years, you will need to adjust your timeline accordingly.

Finally—and of particular interest to most CEOs—is the issue of your own continuation on the board. While the prevailing U.S. sentiment of a decade ago was to allow the former CEO to continue to serve as chairman until he reached the board retirement age—often 72, or even 75—this is no longer a prevalent practice. Boards are sensitive to the challenges for a new CEO trying to take actual leadership of a company with her predecessor sitting in the boardroom; and while most understand the value of keeping the outgoing CEO on as Chairman for some transitional period, that period is now viewed as in the range of six to eighteen months. While there are exceptions—particularly in family-controlled companies, founder scenarios, and other situations in which the outgoing CEO remains one of the company's largest shareholders—for the most part, an outgoing CEO should count on remaining as Chairman for about a year after stepping down. And then moving on, perhaps to serve on some other corporate boards, an issue discussed in the next chapter.

In Summary

Perhaps no aspect of the board and CEO relationship has undergone more substantial change in the past decade than CEO succession planning—arguably, the board's single most important decision. While the succession decision may lie with the board, the CEO—who knows the job and her executive team better than directors ever will—has a crucial role to play in this area.

Emergency CEO Succession Planning

- **Find out what your board has in mind if you were hit by a bus.** Many CEOs are shocked by what they discover. This can help you not only correct misperceptions, but it can kick-start longer-term succession planning discussions in a meaningful way.
- **Put your board in a position to respond within forty-eight hours.** This means driving them to a tentative decision about who the emergency successor will be—recognizing that this decision is never "set in stone," may differ based on actual circumstances of a crisis, and should be reviewed at least annually. Ensure there is also a logistics plan that covers who communicates with which stakeholders when the crisis occurs and in the days and weeks thereafter.
- **Observe the "Las Vegas principle" on emergency CEO succession discussions with the board.** What happens in the boardroom, stays in the boardroom. Don't share it with any of your executives—even if one of them is earmarked as your emergency successor. Doing so creates expectations and inferences that you may regret later on.
- **Expand emergency succession discussions beyond the CEO.** Discuss your readiness and emergency plans in the event that something happened to one of your "mission critical" executives, such as the CFO or a key business unit leader.

RETIREMENT CEO SUCCESSION PLANNING

- **Start by developing and prioritizing the criteria for the next CEO.** This brings objectivity to the succession process before you begin talking about potential candidates. The criteria should reflect the company's business model, strategy, and culture. Engage every member of your board in providing input about the criteria; get similar input from top executives as well.
- **Assess internal candidates against the CEO criteria using three lenses.** The lens of the CEO, the lens of the board, and the lens of a third-party executive assessment professional.
- **Provide board members with meaningful exposure to internal candidates.** Consider vehicles beyond board meetings and dinners.
- **Consider how to best use the COO role.** Will you use the COO role in your succession process largely as a one-year "CEO-in-waiting" position or two-to-three year "proving ground" with significant responsibilities.

CHAPTER 6

SITTING ON ANOTHER COMPANY'S BOARD

WITH CEOS NOW SPENDING UP to a quarter of their time working with their boards individually and collectively,[1] gaining a better understanding of how boards work through actually serving as a director seems an almost obvious step in any CEO's career path. Yet not every CEO takes this step. A 2009 study by Spencer Stuart[2] found that only half of the CEOs of S&P 500 companies serve on other public companies' boards. In fact, some companies actually forbid their CEOs and senior executives from serving on outside boards, citing three main reasons for this position:

- **Time commitment:** On average, directors of public companies spend more than 200 hours a year on board-related business,[3] including preparing for board and committee meetings, attendance at the meetings (including travel to and from them), and participation in a variety of activities outside of meetings, including director education and site visits. This equates to more than two days per month—days that some board members would rather see their CEO and corporate officers devoting to their own company's business.
- **Reputational risk:** An executive's reputation can be severely damaged if the company whose board he chooses to serve on becomes the next Enron or Lehman Brothers. Many directors would prefer not to open up their executive ranks to these types of reputational risks—or risk the reputation of the company itself, which may become similarly impugned through an executive's problematic board association.

- **Executive poaching:** Some directors fear that company officers who serve on other boards may be recruited to those companies either as CEO or in another senior executive role.

Others, however, recognize that sitting on the other side of the board table can be an unparalleled professional-development experience for a CEO or company officer, and they actively encourage their executives to seek out board opportunities. Most CEOs who have had this opportunity describe it as invaluable. Bill Mitchell, Chairman and former CEO of Arrow Electronics, spoke with me about this issue for my column at *Bloomberg* BusinessWeek. A strong advocate of this practice, Mitchell noted that serving on another board gives a CEO "exposure to all the machinery of how a board really works—including committees and executive sessions—which most company executives, particularly those who run business units, never get. But perhaps more important is the insight it gives you on what it feels like to serve in a governance role as opposed to a management role."

If you believe that serving on another board would be beneficial to your career and development as a CEO, the critical first step is to determine which of these two camps your own board members fall into: Are they supporters of the idea who may actually scroll through their BlackBerries' address books to help you find an appropriate board opportunity? Or are they opposed to it altogether?

If the latter, you may be limited to serving on the boards of non-profit organizations. While this can be useful—not to mention personally rewarding—it will not provide you with the same type of exposure to issues that you would receive by serving on a public company board. Nonprofit boards differ in many ways from those of public companies: They have a different focus in terms of their mission, different organizational objectives, and different stakeholders. Many nonprofits have very large boards with executive committees serving in key decision-making roles, a practice curtailed in the public company world nearly a decade ago. The committee structure of nonprofit boards may also differ substantially from that found at public companies. This is not to suggest that nonprofit board service won't be worthwhile—merely that you need recognize some of the differences at the outset.

The majority of boards, however, feel that the benefits of allowing their CEO or other officers to serve on outside public company boards tend to outweigh the risks. Some even become actively involved in trying to place one or more top CEO candidates on other boards as part of their grooming in the CEO succession process. However, even those who embrace the concept typically limit company executives—including the CEO—to only one or two external board seats. It's worth noting also that even boards that generally disapprove of outside directorships sometimes ease their stance on this issue as a CEO approaches retirement, recognizing that outside board service may become a second career for her after she has exited the company.

For an active CEO, a former CEO who remains on as Chairman, or a company executive, it is critical to avoid any potential conflicts of interest when it comes to serving on another board. This will typically mean finding board opportunities outside of your industry and avoiding any directorships involving major customers, suppliers, or other business partners. In today's governance environment, it's wise to take a conservative approach on these issues.

IT'S EASY FOR A CEO TO GET A SEAT ON ANOTHER BOARD, ISN'T IT?

With the press awash with articles lamenting the difficulty in finding new board members, many CEOs and other senior executives assume that they will have little trouble finding good outside board opportunities. The offers should come pouring in, shouldn't they?

You might think so—especially if you review some of the data from Spencer Stuart's 2009 Board Index.[4] This study reports that 49 percent of boards surveyed want to recruit a sitting CEO or COO to their board, and another 34 percent have a retired CEO or COO at the top of their director-recruitment wish list. However, another statistic in that same Spencer Stuart study[5] illustrates that first-time directors—be they sitting CEOs or other top executives—are still challenged when it comes to landing their first directorship: Only 16 percent of new directors appointed to the boards of S&P 500 companies had no previous public company board experience, the smallest percentage in years. Only one year earlier, first-timers accounted for 24 percent of new director appointments; in 2006, 40 percent of new director appointments had no previous board experience.

Bill Mitchell of Arrow Electronics ran into this problem directly when grooming his own successors to become CEO. Mitchell encouraged his top candidates to serve on other boards as part of their professional development; he sat with each of them and explained the time commitment involved in accepting a directorship and the need to avoid any conflicts of interest that might emerge if they were to sit on the boards of other companies in their industry. He urged the candidates to reach out to the major search firms and express interest in being considered for a board appointment. He assumed that his executives would be viewed as excellent board candidates—after all, some were running multibillion-dollar international business units.

The search firms' response astonished Mitchell: They indicated that it would be difficult to find board seats for the top Arrow executives because they had no prior board experience. Surprising as it seemed to Mitchell and his team, this reaction is not atypical. CEOs and other executives across the United States have been reporting a similar response in their overtures to search firms for board opportunities, particularly when they served on no board other than that of their own company. While CEOs with board aspirations should never ignore the search firms or downplay the importance of getting their name into the firms' databases, it is equally important to recognize the need to extend your efforts beyond this traditional route.

Often, the members of your own board can serve as a particularly valuable network in bringing to light other board opportunities. Gone are the days of board interlocks, in which one company's CEO sits on your board and you sit on her board. However, your directors who sit on other boards may be able to tap into that network on your behalf. If you are not yet a CEO and have your boss's support to explore board opportunities, she may pull some strings for you, as Mitchell did for his team. He reached out to some of the strategy consulting firms with which Arrow was working and which he felt might have board-level contacts at other companies. He also spoke up at a meeting of twenty Silicon Valley CEOs, indicating that some of his top executives were interested in board opportunities and providing some background on each: what they'd been doing at Arrow, what their backgrounds were, their areas of expertise, some personal information.

Other CEOs have tapped their external auditors, outside legal counsel, and investment bankers. Contacts in private equity often prove very helpful: Private equity firms are sometimes asked to assemble an entire board—six to eight directors—for an initial public offering, expanding the directorship opportunities available. Sitting CEOs and other active C-suite executives such as COOs and CFOs are often of great interest to companies about to go public, as they are often transitioning some of their venture capitalists off the board and seeking to replace them with directors who bring broad corporate experience.

Regardless of whom you decide to talk to about your interest in serving on another board, it's always best to leverage a network of people who are familiar with you and your capabilities. If they have some insight into a potential board opportunity and decide to put your name forward, they can do so with conviction—you are someone they know or have worked with, or they have received your name from a colleague who has worked with you. This is a far stronger reference that typically carries much more weight than one provided by someone who has only met you socially or briefly at a directors' conference.

Networking is important, but homework can be useful too. One top European executive spent an entire weekend, with sleeves rolled up, looking at companies in the electronics industry—an industry he personally found interesting but that posed no conflict with his current role at a major packaged goods company. With no prior board experience, he recognized that a Fortune 500 company might be out of reach, but a mid cap company might consider him a prize, particularly because he had extensive international experience. To his amazement, he found several mid cap electronics companies with directors who formerly served as executives of his current company. This provided him with an entry point to make contact with some of these people and begin a dialogue.

A Canadian executive who was unable to serve on a public company board took a similar approach to finding a board seat at a major Toronto hospital. She began with research into prominent hospitals in the region, determining their areas of specialty, their size, and what appeared to be their key issues in terms of capital campaigns and other initiatives. From their websites, she compiled a list of all the directors for each hospital that interested her and found that she knew people on three of these boards; in other cases, she "knew someone who would know" one or more of the trustees. Armed with this research, she began making calls. Within six months, she had two board interviews and one board invitation, which she accepted.

PREPARING YOUR BOARD CV

One important tool you will need in your quest to secure a directorship is a CV targeted toward an outside board position, which

---

Box 6.1   Sample Board CV

Jane Doe
85 Canterbury Lane, Seattle, WA 40596
Phone: (444) 555–1212   Email: jdoe@ravenswood.com

Career Summary

Jane Doe is the current Chairman and Chief Executive Officer of Ravenswood Energy, a Nasdaq-listed diversified utility based in the Pacific Northwest with a market cap of approx. $1 billion and annual revenues of approx. $600 million. Jane was hired to Ravenswood as President and Chief Operating Officer in 2005 and appointed Chairman and Chief Executive Officer of the company in 2006. She led the company's initial public offering in 2007. Earlier in her career, Jane held executive positions of increasing responsibility with Mark Power, where she served as the senior officer responsible for the company's largest business unit (with annual revenues of $1.5 billion) and the role of SVP, Strategy.

During her tenure as CEO of Ravenswood, Jane has been involved in two major acquisitions—one involving a wind power producer and the other a mining company based in the Pacific Northwest. She has also become extensively involved in the development of regulatory and political policy within the utility industry. She has served on the Board of the Utilities Institute (UI), a utilities trade association, and played a key role in the review of various energy initiatives proposed by the U.S. House of Representatives and the U.S. Senate on behalf of the Institute.

Jane is one of the only CEOs of a Nasdaq-listed company with experience as a human resources executive, having served as Director of Human Resources and a Manager of Labor Relations and Safety for Mark Power earlier in her career. Jane's HR experience provides unique expertise that can be especially valuable to a board's Human Resources/ Compensation Committee.

Non-Profit Boards/Community Service

Jane has served as campaign cochair of the United Way of greater Seattle, as a member of the Board of Trustees of Cascadian Women's Hospital, and as a Director of Michigan State University.

Education

Jane graduated summa cum laude with a Bachelor of Science from Michigan State and received her Masters of Business Administration from Stanford University.

Personal

Jane and her husband, Frank, have two children and one grandchild.

---

differs in several ways from the traditional CV you've always used. Most executive CVs aim to demonstrate your progression through various levels of increasing responsibility. Typically, they consist of a sequential list of your work history, extending to several pages, giving a brief description of each position—starting with your current or most recent role—and extending back over the previous ten or even twenty years, highlighting your most important accomplishments in each role.

A board CV is an entirely different type of document, focused on establishing your credentials to be an effective director, and typically set out in a narrative format on only one page. For those CEOs who can't abide the thought of providing a CV without a detailed work history, consider attaching this as an appendix. However, don't assume anyone will read it in much detail; you need to make your key points in that one-page narrative.

A sample board CV is provided in box 6.1. As this example illustrates, "Jane" has attempted to highlight those features in her background that make her particularly interesting as a board candidate, including:

- She is the Chairman and CEO of a Nasdaq-listed company.
- She led her company's initial public offering, experience that would be especially attractive to private companies looking to recruit board members in anticipation of an IPO.
- She completed two corporate acquisitions. Many companies whose growth strategy involves M&A activity find this experience invaluable to bring onto their boards—and often prefer a CEO who has been through both M&A negotiations and the process of integrating the companies acquired instead of recruiting an M&A specialist with a legal or investment-banking background.
- She has been extensively involved in political and regulatory issues. As an active CEO, Jane cannot serve on the board of another company in her industry. However, other companies operating in highly regulated industries—such as health care—are likely to find this aspect of her background of great interest. As with M&A, a CEO who brings credentials in this area is often viewed as preferable to a government-relations specialist.
- She has a human resources background from executive roles earlier in her career, making her an ideal candidate to serve on or chair a Compensation Committee.
- Although she has never served on a public company board other than her own, she has served as a director of several non-profit organizations, including a hospital and a university. She is therefore no stranger to the boardroom, even though her experience has been limited to nonprofit board experience to date.

PREPARING FOR YOUR DIRECTOR INTERVIEWS

Up to now, we have focused on steps you can take to generate potential directorship opportunities. Once they begin to emerge, you need to take a somewhat bifurcated approach to your preparation for the next steps—your interviews with directors and the CEO of the company whose board you may be joining. On one hand, you want to convince the board that you would be the best possible candidate. At the same time, accepting any board position carries significant risks in terms of both reputational and financial repercussions. You owe it not only to yourself but also to the company you are leading—whose reputation can be tarnished if you make a bad choice—to do appropriate due diligence on any company interested in discussing a board position.

At the outset of your discussions with the company—and well in advance of your interview—it may be useful to sign a nondisclosure agreement (NDA). If the company doesn't suggest this—and many do not—you may want to raise this issue with them and suggest they send a standard NDA over for you to review and sign. The reason for this is simple: You want the people with whom you are talking in your interviews to be entirely open in sharing all relevant information about the company. If the company is in negotiations to make a major acquisition or to enter into a significant joint venture, you want them to tell you about it, which they may be uncomfortable doing without an NDA in place. You may also wish to request certain information from the company to help you prepare for your interviews—information they might otherwise be reluctant to send you.

Typically, you will receive a packet of information about the company shortly after being contacted about your interest in a board position and, obviously, you will want to review it thoroughly. But you need to extend your research on the company well beyond this: Spend some time on the company's website and research media articles about the company and its CEO. Not only might this alert you to any smoking guns—it will also help you prepare for your upcoming interviews by giving you more things to talk about. One CFO being recruited to chair the Audit Committee of a tech company unearthed a news article indicating that an employee had recently filed an SEC complaint about the company's accounting practices.

If the information packet did not include analysts' reports on the company, ask for them—and then do your own search on analysts' reports to see whether they sent you both the positive and the negative ones. It can also be useful to ask the company to send you any recent strategy road show presentations as well as a couple of board pre-reading packages; the former enables you to have a meatier discussion with the CEO about strategy issues, while the latter gives you insight into the quality of information that directors regularly receive to prepare for meetings. It doesn't hurt to ask for next year's board schedule too, to see if there are any conflicts with your own board meetings or other commitments. If this is a serious problem, you may need to withdraw your candidacy immediately or ask to postpone joining the board until after the dates where these conflicts occur.

One of the challenges for any sitting CEO or other senior executive interested in a board position is the need to avoid conflicts of interest, which necessitates going outside of your industry to find a suitable board position. This factor compounds the challenges in preparing for your interview on both fronts: Because you are less familiar with this company's line of business, not only do you need to climb the learning curve on a new industry, but warning signs of potential problems may be less apparent. I've helped more than one CEO solve this problem by making an introduction to another CEO in the industry in which the board he's being recruited for operates. Similarly, if you have, or can make, any industry contacts, you may find these conversations extremely helpful. Obviously, you need to be careful not to violate any of the terms of the NDA you just signed, but indicating that you are in preliminary discussions about a potential board opportunity and asking general questions about the company's reputation and that of its CEO and senior management is generally appropriate—and can be extremely illuminating.

The interview format and the order in which you will meet the different players vary widely from company to company. In most cases, you will meet initially with the Lead Director and/or someone from the Nominating/Governance Committee. Typically, a meeting with the CEO follows this initial discussion. After that, you may meet other members of the board as well; some boards invite their director candidates to the start or end of a board meeting, where they sit down to a discussion with the entire board en masse or join a board dinner. There is nothing unusual about any of these practices; since 2003, when Nominating/Governance Committees assumed responsibility for director recruitment, boards have experimented with a variety of formats in terms of director interviews.

Some of the key questions for which you may want to be prepared in either of your interviews include:

- **Why do you want to serve on a board—and why our board?** Don't be shy about saying that you are looking for the experience of sitting on the other side of the board table. That's why many active CEOs and top executives accept outside directorships. However, you obviously need to go beyond this issue and talk about what interests you about this particular company. If you've done your homework, you should have no problem making two or three good points in answering this question—and in doing so, you can demonstrate your preparation. You might also want to mention the fact that because you are a sitting CEO or executive, your own board will limit you to one outside board, and you need to choose that board carefully. Then cite two or three reasons why you feel this is the right board opportunity for you, based on your research.

- **How have you handled a situation involving ethical concerns?** This was a popular director-recruitment question following the scandals at Enron, Tyco, WorldCom, and other companies in 2001–2003. Many board members still have this question—or a variation of it—on their list, so be prepared for it, with an example at the ready that you are comfortable sharing.

- **What do you see as the most important issue in governance today?** Some question about governance is likely to emerge in the interviews. It is often posed as a technical question, to see if you are keeping abreast of new SEC rules and other developments in governance regulations or similar trends. You may, therefore, want to allude to some recent governance developments, even if your actual answer aims elsewhere. For example, "Say on Pay has been a hot topic in the compensation arena for the past two years, but I really think a far more important issue is the way in which boards and CEOs work together on succession planning."

- **What contribution do you believe that you can make to our board?** This provides you with a wonderful opportunity to showcase the way in which your background and experience can add significant value for this company, its shareholders, and fellow directors. While the question may seem like an easy one, it is so important that it is worth taking some time to prepare your answer in advance.

If board members are spread out in different geographic locations, some interviews may be conducted by telephone. If this is the case, ensure that there are two interviews conducted in person no matter what: the interviews with the CEO and with the Lead Director or Nonexecutive Chair. These are the two most essential interviews in the entire process—with the leader of the company and the leader of the independent directors. Not only will these yield the most valuable insights in terms of the tone at the top of both the company and the board, but these two people are typically the most important decision-makers in terms of a board invitation. If you are being recruited to chair a particular board committee—current or former CFOs being asked to chair the Audit Committee is the most frequent example—you should also meet with the Audit Committee Chair as part of your interview process. It may also be useful to meet with the CFO and even the external auditors as discussions progress.

Your meeting with the CEO will probably be the most pivotal of all of your discussions in terms of your decision whether to accept an invitation to join this board. Prospective director candidates who are sitting or former CEOs have a decided advantage in this conversation: You can imagine yourself in the other CEO's position, which is exactly what you should do in preparing for this important interview.

While CEOs are typically enthusiastic about the prospect of having another CEO join their board, their reservations about this are generally twofold:

- First, they question whether another active CEO will be willing and able to make the time to prepare for board meetings and give the affairs of the company proper share of mind, given the responsibilities she is already shouldering at her own company.
- Second, as with any director who lacks an industry background, they are concerned about the new director's willingness to devote the time and effort required to become knowledgeable about the industry and its issues. Many CEOs tell me, "I expect my directors to learn about our industry and keep abreast of developments in that industry. This requires considerable effort on their part

if they have no industry background. However, I think it's fair to expect them to make that effort if they are going to be on the board of this company. They will be making critical decisions that will significantly impact the company and how it operates."

The best way to offset these concerns is to prepare some questions that will subtly but clearly let the CEO know that you have not only read the materials in your information packet but have taken the time to go beyond them in your research about the company and its industry. This demonstrates your commitment to prepare properly and learn about the industry.

You should also plan some questions that will give you useful insights into the working relationship between the CEO and the board, such as:

- *What does the CEO see as the board's strengths? What are some of the contributions that the board has made to the company and where have they added value for him, personally, as CEO?* Every board has its strengths, and if the CEO refuses to acknowledge any of them, this suggests a strained relationship that you may not want to become a part of. Even short of this, if the CEO appears dismissive of the board in his answers, this could be a big red flag suggesting that you might find this working relationship a frustrating one.
- *What does the CEO see as the priorities for the company and for the board over the next six, twelve, and eighteen months?* This is a good question to ask in your interviews both with the directors and with the CEO, to confirm that they align on priority issues. It will also give you a sense of the most important issues with which you will be dealing upon joining the board. Moreover, it can be useful to see whether the CEO is able to discern between a company priority and a board priority, which can provide further insights into how he views the role of the board.
- *Where could the board be more effective than it is today? Could it make a greater contribution, and if so, in what ways?* Obviously, if the CEO is at a loss to suggest any improvements to the board, you know that she is not being frank with you. What you are looking to determine is whether she—possibly like yourself—is actually looking to get greater value from her board by recruiting new directors who can help the board to raise its game. If you

get this sense from her, this may be a board opportunity you will really enjoy.

There is no question that serving on another company's board will require a significant commitment in terms of time, effort, and scheduling—even finding an appropriate board opportunity may require some legwork. Taking a seat in another company's boardroom can be daunting. You need to be willing to make that commitment—in the same way that you would expect anyone serving on your board to do. If you can't, it's best not to sign up. Moreover, board work isn't for everyone; some CEOs who join another board are initially frustrated to find that their view in the boardroom is only one of many, and it may be accepted or rejected by the others. That said, few CEOs or senior executives who have had the opportunity to serve on an outside public company board have not found it to be an enlightening and important experience in their professional development.

IN SUMMARY

Sitting on the other side of the board table can be an unparalleled professional development experience for CEOs and other executives. If your goal is to secure a directorship opportunity at another public company, these steps may help you to find the right one:

- **Ensure your board's support.** While most boards see directorship experience as beneficial and encourage their executives in this regard, some forbid it. Determine your board's position on this issue at the outset.
- **Expand your efforts beyond traditional routes.** Don't limit your outreach to search firms; actively tap the networks of your own directors, strategy consultants, lawyers, auditors, and the like. Do some homework to identify companies that may interest you— and where you may have contacts.
- **Avoid conflicts of interest.** This will likely mean finding board opportunities outside of your industry and avoiding any directorships involving major customers, suppliers, and the like.
- **Develop a Board CV.** This consists of a one-page narrative highlighting those features of your background that would make you particularly attractive as a board candidate.

- **Prepare for your director interviews.** Do so by extending your research into the company well beyond the packet of materials you will be sent. Look at analysts' reports, press releases, and media articles; make some calls to contacts you may have in the industry. Ask questions to give you insights into the relationship between the board and the CEO.

CHAPTER 7

As You Move Forward . . .

MANY CEOS SAY THAT THEY WANT TO CHANGE THEIR BOARDS to derive more value from them, but often find it difficult to achieve this. Three of the most common reasons that their efforts prove unsuccessful are: (1) A failure to understand and address all eight components that factor into board effectiveness. (2) Asking for greater openness between the board and CEO but responding in a way that is defensive or critical when you get it. (3) Delegation of board changes that require leadership from the CEO.

1. **A failure to understand and address all eight components that factor into board effectiveness:** The most common approach to addressing board issues involves the tweaking of one or two elements—such as replacing a new director or adopting a popular "best practice" such as the formation of a Risk Committee—only to find that impact of these initiatives on the overall functioning of the board is marginal, at best. Simultaneously tackling all eight components is nearly impossible: changing board composition, how the board engages in strategy and succession, the way board agendas are designed, the information packages directors receive and the orientation for new board members, how board and committee meetings are led, and so on. However, if you limit your efforts to only one or two areas, you will never maximize the board's potential.

Similarly, there are many instances of CEOs who create lists of board expectations or tell the board how they want to engage with them differently—yet do nothing in terms of active steps that will facilitate this. They may have said that they want and value more constructive board dialogue, yet they continue to send out poorly organized pre-reading packages that lack essential information, create agendas that no board could get through in a week much less a few hours, and fail to draw out different perspectives from their directors during the discussions.

One CEO described exactly these frustrations earnestly and sincerely: "I have told them I want to work with them differently than my predecessor did. I laid it all out in a concise slide that I sent out in the pre-reading packages and talked about with the entire board at the end of one of our meetings. But nothing has changed." Of course nothing had changed. He had done nothing to change any of the essential components of how the board was operating. Once we began to analyze and address all eight components, the deficiencies became apparent very quickly: Among other things, this company was involved extensively in acquisitions. Ad hoc board meetings were often called at the last minute to talk about deals—often by conference call; advance materials were slim due to time constraints. Moreover, the company had entered two new lines of business in a significant way over the past five years, yet no board members had been recruited with experience in these industries. It had been so long since any directors had joined the board, in fact, there was no orientation program that anyone could remember.

Changes began by scheduling one board meeting per month, some by conference call. Up to this point, only five regular board meetings a year were scheduled; when, in fact, the board had "met" more than ten times in each of the previous two years to discuss and approve major transactions. With monthly meetings now scheduled, the panic of trying to track down directors for urgent approvals of pending transactions subsided. In fact, some of these monthly board meetings were ultimately cancelled; but having them in place in this company's operating environment made a big difference.

Another significant change involved the way deals were presented in the pre-reading materials and the establishment of a rule that some sort of pre-reading—even on forty-eight to seventy-two hours notice—was to be provided before *all* meetings or board conference calls. Board members were frustrated with the lack of information relative to matters for discussion on urgent board calls. As one director described it, "I get on that call and I have some idea what we're going to talk about but can I say I feel well-informed about it? Absolutely not! I feel like my back is against the wall—if I hesitate or start asking questions, it is like, 'What's wrong with you? We need a decision from the board right now! You are holding management back and we need to move! Don't you get it?'"

In two instances where time was particularly short, rather than create pre-reading, the CEO told directors that he was arranging two different times when they could dial into conference calls two days prior to the board meeting itself for a briefing. In these preliminary calls, his deal team would outline the essentials of the transaction and provide directors with the overview they would otherwise have received in the pre-reading. This proved to be a very workable solution for both the directors and the management team: In both instances the board approved the deal in record time when the meeting, itself, occurred.

The Nominating/Governance Committee began recruitment efforts to find two directors who provided backgrounds in the new lines of business. Initially, there was reluctance to expand the size of the board—particularly given the frequency of discussions. Even the CEO expressed concerns: "I have seven people on the board now, and I think it would work even better if there were only five. We are talking about an increase to nine. I don't like that idea." However, no one was nearing retirement and, despite all the meetings, no one wanted to leave. While two were clearly stars, even among the other five no one was an obvious choice to remove from the board.

The CEO began to realize that his alternatives were limited: He could continue with the seven directors he had or could expand the board to nine and bring on some people with backgrounds in the new businesses. He opted for the latter—and was very glad he did. The new directors were invaluable not only in board discussions but also as a resource to the CEO between meetings. These lines of business were new to him, too; he valued the perspective his new board members provided. This was particularly important because the two new areas of business were essential to the company's overall growth strategy.

To integrate the new board recruits quickly—and ensure that they understood the company's core business—a comprehensive board orientation program was developed by the corporate secretary and the Nominating/Governance Committee with input from the CEO. It was so good, in fact, that longer-serving directors asked if they could go through the program.

Members of the company's executive team were thrilled with the changes: "This board has been reinvigorated in the past year. They are really helping us—and not just the new directors, who have been very important additions—but the others, too. Our board meetings are a lot more productive now—and far more enjoyable. I used to hate going to board meetings. It was like the Spanish Inquisition in there; now it's like a think tank. That doesn't mean they don't wrestle stuff to the ground with us; in fact, they do it more. They've said no to two of our deals in the past nine months. And you know—all gnashing of teeth aside—I really think they were right about those two; one of them, in particular, where we really were being pushed by the bankers."

2. **Asking for greater openness between the board and CEO—but responding in a way that is defensive or critical when you get it:** When board members and the CEO discuss their working relationship, they typically indicate a desire for openness, a relationship in which both parties are candid in their discussions and never hesitate to say what's really on their minds. Outlining these expectations is one thing, but following through on it often proves challenging—for both sides.

One CEO who experienced these types of frustrations had recently replaced a founder at a rapidly growing professional services company. The board was largely populated with friends of the founder; a few more recent additions from outside the state had added some degree of independence and deepened the board's financial acumen. However, this was a board that seldom raised any significant challenges—or provided the management team with many insights at all.

The new CEO felt that board members could make a much stronger contribution than they had under his predecessor's regime. It was clear to him that many directors were holding back from expressing their views in board meetings. "In the meetings, they hardly say anything worthwhile" he told me. "Yet, when I have spoken with some of them privately afterwards, they will quietly tell me some of the questions they really had about an issue—but never raised."

To set these changes in motion, the new CEO sat down at the end of a board meeting and talked about changes he wanted to see in the board and CEO relationship. He had met with each director individually and felt confident that they would welcome this new approach. Indeed, his remarks were greeted with enthusiasm. Everyone left the boardroom feeling that an exciting new era had begun. Yet, nine months later, the CEO was completely frustrated. "Nothing has changed", he complained. "I felt really good when we all came out of that meeting. And I did notice slightly more openness in the board discussions right after that. But that's all tapered off now; it's back to the way it was before, when Roger was CEO. I think they became so used to operating that way under Roger's leadership that they can't really make the changes I had been hoping for."

As we began interviewing board members, however, their perspective on what had happened was quite different. One director told us, "We were excited when Ken sat down and told the board that he wanted to work with us differently than Roger had. He told us that he wanted us to really challenge him—to dig in and offer our best thinking. But that sure didn't last long. At the very next meeting, Ken wanted to make some major investments on the West Coast. We'd been having problems out there for years. So, the directors began to raise a number of concerns about whether this was really the right direction to go. Well, it turned out Ken wasn't too keen about having the board challenge his ideas after all. He got incredibly defensive. Later in the meeting, someone brought up an issue that wasn't on the agenda about a potential joint venture we'd been looking at in Europe. There had been a big article in the *Financial Times* about our joint venture partner that wasn't too flattering. Ken shut that discussion down altogether. When I was heading to the airport with two other directors we began joking—so much for the era of good feelings in the boardroom."

The new CEO took the director's comments to heart. He addressed the situation directly at the next meeting—with just his board members in the room. He jokingly acknowledged his defensiveness and asked if they could give it another try. He also sat down with his Lead Director and discussed the situation. Among other things, he was disappointed that the Lead Director hadn't told him the board's perspective on this issue, emphasizing that he wanted her candid feedback going forward.

The Lead Director gave the CEO some direct coaching right in their meeting: "At the last meeting, Carlos clearly had a concern about the leadership changes you were making in the sales division. It was written all over his face. What you should have done is asked him directly to express his view. Read the body language and draw people into the conversation—especially where it's evident that something is bothering them. You can say, 'Well, it's up to them,' but if you really want to demonstrate a desire for openness and challenge, you have to take some steps to reinforce this. Otherwise, board members may not feel that these types of challenges really are welcome, no matter what you may have said to them."

Slowly, changes began to take hold. Six months later the CEO had already noticed a difference: "Sometimes I wonder if I should have told them to challenge me quite so much," he joked, "It can get uncomfortable at times. But the truth is, even in the last six months, there have been some points that the board has made which really helped my thinking about some important issues. That's what I wanted, and now I'm starting to get it—so, it's been worth it. This board has added more value to me in the past six months than I've seen in the previous three years that I've been working with them."

It is worth noting that this problem cuts both ways: It can be the board that behaves in a manner that causes the CEO to be less than open. A good example occurred with the board and CEO of a financial services company. In this instance, the board emphasized the importance of the CEO being entirely open in sharing bad news— particularly in the aftermath of the 2008 meltdown in the industry, which this company had managed to weather. "If there is even a specter of a problem, we want to know about it," directors told the CEO. "Don't try to keep it from us, hoping the problem will go away over time. These problems never do; they just get worse. So, the sooner you let us know about a potential problem, the better."

The CEO took the board's message to heart. A few months after this conversation there was, in fact, some bad news to share. The situation hadn't yet become a serious problem, but the CEO felt he would share it with the board in the spirit of honoring the open relationship they had discussed. Almost immediately, he came to regret that decision. The reaction of the board was intense, critical, and bordered on panic. "I realize that there is a lot of sensitivity to any potential problem right now," the CEO explained. "That's why I decided to tell them that there *may* be a problem, although we were still investigating it. But they went nuts. It was totally over the top! I expected them to commend me for being open in giving them a heads-up. Instead, I walked out of that meeting feeling like my days were numbered."

The CEO scheduled dinner with the Presiding Director to discuss the situation and found a good ally. "You're right," the Presiding Director told him. "We told you to share even the specter of bad news with us. So, you did—and then we practically crucified you. If I were you, I wouldn't share any bad news with this board ever again. But that's obviously not what we want, so we need to talk about how to handle this better." At the next meeting, the Presiding Director led a discussion in an executive session and brought the board to agreement on how to handle these types of situations. He then debriefed with the CEO and told him, "We agreed that if we want you to be open with us, our first reaction should be to appreciate your openness. Our next reaction should be to help you wrestle with the problem—can we offer suggestions that might be helpful? Obviously, if it is bad news item after bad news item, that's a different situation—but that's not at all what we have."

In the end, investigations proved that the suspected problem that triggered this incident was insignificant. The CEO noted: "Some people might say that I should never have raised this matter with the board in the first place. It caused a lot of grief, and the entire issue became a 'nonevent.' However, it became a vehicle to discuss our working relationship—and that was actually very helpful. The board has been true to their word. I brought up some problematic issues with them again, almost to test the waters. Their reaction was quite different this time: They asked me what my alternatives were and we discussed a Plan B and Plan C if the problem actually materialized. One director even offered to make a call to one of his contacts that might be able to help."

3. **Delegation of board changes that require leadership from the CEO:** With so many demands on the time of a CEO, delegation is always essential. However, as with many facets of corporate leadership, trying to delegate some of the fundamental components of board leadership can result in a situation where many of your initiatives simply fail to get off the ground.

One of the most common problems involves tasking the corporate secretary with responsibility for board pre-reading materials and the board agenda and then walking away from those issues almost entirely. Some CEOs never even read the board packets until they have already gone out to their directors. If there are deficiencies in these materials, it is too late to correct them; any shortcomings will need to be addressed in the board meeting, itself, taking up valuable time. The board agenda is often left entirely to the corporate secretary as well—with merely a cursory review and a few additions by the CEO and Lead Director. Yet both of these elements—pre-reading materials and agenda design—are critical to the effectiveness of your board meetings. Any CEO who is serious about deriving greater value from the board needs to take an active role in making changes in these areas—at least at the outset. After new practices have effectively taken root, delegating to the corporate secretary to help stay the course is fine.

This means taking the time to review the board book before it is finalized—doing so sufficiently far in advance that if, for example, executive summaries on agenda items are weak or confusing you can call up the responsible executives and correct the problem. It can also be an interesting exercise to create a first draft of an upcoming board agenda—fashioning it the way you would really like to run the meeting and breaking old patterns. Often, board agendas look like they have been almost unchanged from something developed in about the mid–1980s. Design the agenda with a view to achieving a 50/50 balance of presentation and discussion time and focusing on three or four of the critical issues at the front end, while directors are fresh. Then, give that draft agenda to your corporate secretary to flesh out, and to your Lead Director to review. See if it doesn't result in a more energized meeting environment than has been created in the past.

Some CEOs like to conduct a run-through of the entire board meeting with their executives a day or two in advance. This can be an extremely useful practice, particularly when you are trying to create improvements. Right away you will see where the discussion is likely to become bogged down in details, or where a particular presentation may lull the board to sleep. This enables you to make changes that will lead to far more effective meetings. It may not be necessary to follow this practice every time, but when you are focused on heightening the effectiveness of your board and its meetings, this can be a useful exercise.

It's important to factor your executive team into the boardroom equation. Most executives—and most CEOs for that matter—are not trained on how to be effective in working with a board. They learn from watching their bosses—picking up good and bad habits in the process. Make sure to give your executives feedback on how they are coming across in board meetings—reinforcing what they're doing well and making suggestions for improvement. Consider asking the board for their comments on the management presentations at the end of every board meeting, and passing these on to your executives. Directors' perceptions of an executive's boardroom capabilities are important; among other things, they can become a significant factor in succession planning discussions. One CEO of a health care company held a half-day governance tutorial for his entire executive team shortly after the company's IPO, explaining, "I wanted to give all of my senior management an overview on how boards work so that they fully understand the context in which they will now be working with our board as a public company." Others have offered coaching to some of their top executives who lack strong presentation skills or seem uncomfortable responding to board questions during the meetings.

Leadership issues extend to board meetings, themselves, where the quality of discussion and decision making is often directly related to the Chairman's skills in running the meeting. Most CEOs learn how to run board meetings by watching their predecessors—or by watching another Chairman do it, if they have an opportunity to serve on an outside board. If you are serving as Chairman and CEO—the predominant model in the United States—it's important to recognize that chairing board meetings requires ability as a facilitator. One CEO who had recently been given the Chairman's title received some useful feedback from her Presiding Director after her second meeting as Chairman: "When you are Chair of the Board, your head has to be up—not down. After you introduce each topic, you look down at your materials, either taking notes or preparing for what you are going to say next. This is perfectly okay when you are just CEO. But as Chair, you need to watch what's going on around that board table so that you can actively manage the meeting—draw people out, shut down conversation that is taking the discussion off topic, call the question at the right time. You are not doing that. Your head is down; you are preparing for the discussion of the next agenda item. You need to get your head up and actively direct our meetings. It requires you to be a little bit ambidextrous between the Chair and CEO roles."

In another instance, the CEO of a pharmaceutical company had been lobbying the Lead Director about asking one board member, who said very little in meetings, for her resignation. During a discussion in which the CEO again raised this issue, the Lead Director told him, "You know, you are the Chairman of the Board. Yet you never confront Sylvia and force her to express an opinion in our meetings; you just let her sit there and say nothing. Then you complain about it. At the next meeting, we are going to discuss a patent issue and that's a topic that she ought to be pretty conversant about, given her legal background.

Why don't you ask her directly what she thinks about this issue? Don't single her out—ask some other people too—but force her to express an opinion."

The CEO took the Lead Director's advice. As discussion ensued on the patent problem, he watched Sylvia looking out the boardroom window, distracted. Finally he said, "Sylvia, given your background in patent litigation, I think we could all benefit from your perspectives on this issue. What do you think?" Sylvia turned and responded, "Oh, I pretty much agree with what's been said so far." Following the meeting, the Lead Director said he was now willing to sit down with Sylvia and discuss her future as a director—or lack of it. Sylvia left the board.

There is no substitute for leadership—and any change initiative, be it within your company or within your board, is largely doomed without leadership. If you want to lead your board—and lead it to a greater level of overall effectiveness—achieving this requires your active involvement.

BOARDROOM TRUST-BREAKERS

Early on in this book, the importance of building a relationship of trust between the board and the CEO was underscored. Many of the initiatives outlined can serve to foster that trust, but none are likely to be successful if trust becomes damaged. Here, then, are some of the most common trust-breakers between boards and CEOs that I have observed over the years—pitfalls that CEOs can sometimes fall into without even recognizing the problem, or understanding its magnitude on their ongoing relationship with the board.

THE GARDEN OF EDEN

This is a situation in which everything is always presented to the board as positive and wonderful; there is never any bad news to share. If there appears to be a problem or concern, it is dismissed quickly rather than addressed directly. "These board meetings are like a trip to Disneyland," a director once told me, with regard to working with a CEO who took this approach. "Everything's always great here in the Magic Kingdom. None of the rides are ever broken or have long lines.

Indeed, our stock has performed extremely well so, obviously, the CEO is doing something right. However, I've been around long enough to know that there are problems and headaches that accompany every success. But we never hear much about those. When the board does start asking questions, trying to pinpoint where some problems might lie, the CEO immediately becomes defensive and tries to change the topic. All this does is create suspicion. Maybe things really are just fine; but his demeanor suggests that he's hiding something. And I'll tell you, if and when the problems begin to emerge, this board will show no mercy."

ONLY ONE SOLUTION—MY SOLUTION

In this instance, the CEO has a pattern of coming to the board with only one recommendation for an item being proposed—his recommendation. The focus of the entire presentation is on why this is such a good idea and why the board needs to approve it immediately. While most boards expect a CEO to come into the board meeting with a point of view on every issue, they object to this single-minded approach. "When the CEO makes a proposal to us, he never talks about what the alternatives are," one director explains. "He only drives home what it is that he thinks we need to do. I respect the fact that he's formed an opinion, and I'm sure it's well-considered. I want him to come to us with a recommendation—that's his job. Nonetheless, I'd like to know what the other options were—and why the CEO dismissed them. Just give me some balance on your decision making. There is never only one solution. But that's all we ever hear about. If someone asks, "Are there any alternatives?" the reply is always, "None that are worth talking about."

A related, but more insidious, problem involves the CEO's failure to fully discuss the implications of her proposal with the board. Only later, as she moves forward into execution, do these implications emerge, and the board feels blindsided by the fact that she failed to outline them when she initially asked for their approval. "I'll tell you why I don't trust her anymore," a director noted about a CEO who had fallen into this trap. "She told us she had signed this supplier contract and that it was a minor amount of money. It was. But what she didn't tell us is that the first contract obligated the company to enter into more contracts with that supplier year after year—and the total amount was very significant. Only when quality problems emerged with this supplier's products, was the full extent of this contractual obligation revealed to the board. So, the CEO's been on shaky ground with me—and with all of us—ever since."

HEARD IT THROUGH THE GRAPEVINE

The classic statement on board communication has always been that directors should never learn about an important development at the company by reading it in the morning newspaper. Communication between the CEO and board is the very cornerstone of that relationship; it deserves proper attention and consideration. By no means should the CEO be calling up directors on a weekly basis just to "say Hi"—it makes them wonder if he doesn't have better things to do. However, when significant issues arise, the CEO needs to stand back and consider whether and how best to let directors know about them. Even something quite subtle can have an impact: "I learned yesterday in our board meeting that we were doing a bond issue," the director of an NYSE-listed company told me. "I think that's great; I've been harping on capital structure for years. But I noticed in the meeting that several of the other directors were clearly not hearing about this for the first time. And, hey! I spent twenty-five years of my life on Wall Street. When you recruited me to the board, you told me you wanted my insights on finance issues. So why would you bother calling me about a bond issue? I mean, I would have no worthwhile comments to add."

LET THEM EAT CAKE

This refers to a CEO who is either outwardly dismissive and disrespectful toward board members, or—the more common scenario—one who says all the right things about wanting to partner with the board and listen to their sage advice but comes across as entirely insincere in this regard. Small indicators like a failure to return directors' calls, inattention during meetings, and other signals that the board is clearly at the bottom of the CEO's list of priorities are seldom missed by those on the receiving end. Perhaps one of the more extreme examples involved a CEO who told the board, "Hey, I'm tired of your grumbling. If you don't like what I've been doing, you can fire me. I don't need this job." They did.

A more subtle example: "At the last meeting, we got into a big discussion about a joint venture in Canada," a director whose CEO had also taken this approach explained. "Many of the board members were making some really good points about this thing. And what was he doing through this entire debate? He was in a sidebar conversation with his CFO or looking at his BlackBerry. Then he looks up with this kind of phony smile and says, "That was really helpful. Thank you." Yeah, right. He wasn't listening to anything we had to say. He'd made up his mind about what he was doing in Canada, and he was just going through the motions of letting us feel we'd had some input. But everybody saw through it and was completely turned off. That night at the board dinner, nobody wanted to sit next to him."

Two Great Things About Working with Your Board

Now that we've canvassed a number of things that can impede your progress in maximizing your board's potential, and can undermine the trust required for an effective board relationship, let's focus on a couple of things that are really great about working with your board:

- **Experimentation is perfectly okay.** One of the things I most enjoy about working in the field of governance is that it evolves almost daily. Certainly, boards operate within a regulatory structure prescribed by Sarbanes-Oxley, the SEC, the rules of the stock exchanges, and other provisions, but within that structure there is a very wide berth to experiment with the way that you work with your board. And I'd encourage you to do exactly that: experiment. Boards often fall into patterns that persist for years—sometimes decades. Break them, if they're not working. Try an executive session at the start of the board meeting instead of at the end. Revamp your board agenda. Consider new approaches to board site visits or strategy offsites. Today's new boardroom experiment is tomorrow's best practice. Don't get mired in best practices, either. If it doesn't make sense to separate the roles of Chairman and CEO, don't do it. If your Audit Committee is overseeing risk issues just fine, leave them there. Create a Strategy Committee, if it suits your needs—and disband it when it doesn't. Try out a director peer review or a new process for CEO evaluation. Resist the all-too-prevalent temptation to treat the board as an area where all practices are prescribed and unchangeable. Seek ways to make your board more energized, more engaged, and more fun.

- **When you get it right, you will have created a significant asset at the very top of the company.** Earlier today, I spoke to a CEO who inherited a troubled board from his predecessor several years ago. Since that time, he's addressed those difficult issues and made other important changes in how he works with the board. Three new directors with stunning credentials have also been recruited. In the past year alone, his board's advice and support helped him as he moved forward in the negotiation of significant transactions with major industry players and in taking a difficult and somewhat emotional step that was required in the interests of cost-cutting. In the last board evaluation, new directors said that this was far and away the best board they'd ever worked with or served on, and longer-serving board members and executives told him this was the best board the company has ever had. His experience illustrates the difference that an inspired CEO can make in the boardroom, what can be achieved, and the types of benefits that can result from your efforts. Today, when so many CEOs are being asked to do more with less, why overlook the value that lies untapped at the very top of your company? When you get it right, you will have created a significant asset.

IN SUMMARY

Many CEOs say that they want to change their boards to derive more value from them, but often find it difficult to achieve this. Three of the most common reasons that their efforts prove unsuccessful are:

- **A failure to understand and address all eight components that factor into board effectiveness.** It's critical to examine all eight components that factor into board effectiveness and address each one to maximize the board's potential and create meaningful boardroom change.
- **Asking for greater openness between the board and CEO, but responding in a way that is defensive or critical when you get it.** If you tell the board that you want them to challenge you, yet

react defensively when they do, it won't take long for them to revert to their previous patterns.

- **Delegation of board changes that require leadership from the CEO.** Trying to delegate fundamental components of board leadership can result in a situation in which many of your initiatives simply fail to get off the ground.

Building trust with the board is the most critical underpinning of your relationship with them. Some common pitfalls that can damage trust include:

- Presenting everything to the board in a positive light and seldom mentioning any negatives or downsides. Before long, the board becomes skeptical and begins to wonder what you're hiding.
- Pushing something through for board approval without discussing the potential downsides, implications, and alternatives. Directors feel blindsided when consequences emerge during implementation that they had no idea might result.
- Failing to communicate with board members—as a group or individually—about significant company developments. Directors—or some of them—seem to be the last to know.
- Treating board members in a dismissive or disrespectful way— either overtly or subtly—by making it evident that you're not listening to, or interested in, what they have to say.

Two great things about working with your board:

- **Experimentation is perfectly okay.** Although boards operate within a regulatory structure, there is still a wide berth to change and experiment in the way you work with your board within that structure. Today's new boardroom experiment is tomorrow's best practice. Seek ways to make your board more energized, more engaged and more fun.
- **When you get it right, you will have created a significant asset at the very top of the company.** Today, when so many CEOs are being asked to do more with less, why overlook the value that lies untapped at the very top of your company? When you get it right, you will have created a significant asset for your company, your shareholders, your executive team, and yourself.

Notes

Introduction: Welcome to the Boardroom

1. Braksick, Leslie W., and, James S. Hillgren. "Preparing CEOs for Success: What I Wish I Knew." CEO study sponsored by William R. Johnson, Chairman, President, and CEO of H.J. Heinz Company; The Continuous Learning Group, 2010, p. 140.
2. 2009 Public Company Governance Survey, National Association of Corporate Directors, p. 13. (*Note: In the 2010 NACD Public Company Governance Survey, questions that asked directors to rate their boards' effectiveness overall and on specific issues were eliminated.*)
3. Meyer, Keith B., and Robert S. Rollo. "Boards Think They're Doing a Good Job. . . . But CEOs Disagree." Boardmember.com, August 2008.

1   Boardroom Priorities for New CEOs

1. 2009 Spencer Stuart Board Index, p. 21.
2. 2009 Spencer Stuart Board Index, p. 22.

2   Strategy—The First Big Test with Your Board

1. 2010 Public Company Governance Survey, National Association of Corporate Directors, p. 10; 2009 Public Company Governance Survey, National Association of Corporate Directors, p. 12.
2. 2009 Public Company Governance Survey, National Association of Corporate Directors, p. 13. Note: Questions on board effectiveness were not included in the 2010 NACD Public Company Governance Survey.

6 SITTING ON ANOTHER COMPANY'S BOARD

1. Leslie W. Braksick and James S. Hillgren, "Preparing CEOs for Success: What I Wish I Knew." CEO study sponsored by William R. Johnson, Chairman, President, and CEO of H.J. Heinz Company; The Continuous Learning Group, 2010, p. 140.
2. 2009 Spencer Stuart Board Index, p. 19.
3. 2010 Public Company Governance Survey, National Association of Corporate Directors, p. 14.
4. 2009 Spencer Stuart Board Index, p. 15.
5. Ibid., p. 12.

INDEX